History and Archaeology of Eritrea

From Earliest Time to Medieval Period

History and Archaeology of Eritrea

From Earliest Time to Medieval Period

Raman Kumar Soni

Kaveri Books
New Delhi-110002

First Published in 2013
ISBN 978-81-7479-150-4

Published by
Kaveri Books
4832/24, Ansari Road
New Delhi - 110 002 (India)
Tel.: 011-2328 8140, 2324 5799
E-mail: kaveribooks@vsnl.com,
kaveribooks@gmail.com
Website: www.kaveribooks.com

Laser Typesetting by : Deep Graphics, Delhi

PRINTED IN INDIA

Dedicated To

My Family Members and Beloved Students

With Lots of Love

Contents

Preface

The present work "History and Archaeology of Eritrea: From Earliest Time to Medieval Period" is a dream come true. It's a fruit of my five years of intensive work. I had some knowledge of Eritrean history and archaeology by virtue of specializing on African history during my M.Phil study. But, I got deeply interested in it after joining Department of History, College of Arts and Social Sciences (CASS), Eritrea as faculty member in 2008. Fortunately, I got ample opportunity to teach and practice African history.

One day, I came to know about "Ona Culture" during a casual discussion with my local colleague. I was informed about the tremendous effort made by Peter Schmidt, M. Curtis, and their students (part of Archaeology Department in Asmara University) in this context. This aroused immense curiosity about Eritrean history and archaeology.

Then all of sudden, I came across an archaeological site within the campus of Eritrea Institute of Technology (EIT) Mai-Nefi. I observed the site and surroundings and planned to do some researches on it. Dr. T. Vijay Kumar, Head, Department of History in CASS further motivated and pushed me to do so. I began getting acquainted with Eritrean history and archaeology. In the meantime, the useful interaction with Dr. Krishna Rao (Head, Department of Anthropology and Archaeology in CASS) also enlightened and provoked me. Somehow my plan to work on aforesaid site could not materialize due to some or the other reasons. But, I could not resist my temptation to know more and more about Eritrean history and archaeology.

So, I decided to collect some data. The first obvious place to look over was the library of CASS. To my great dismay, I could not find a good book on Eritrean history. Then I decided to search libraries and archives in Asmara (capital city of Eritrea). Once again, I came across the moment of disappointment. I could lay hands on some books on Eritrean colonial history and freedom struggle. But, there was not even a single authoritative work on ancient and medieval Eritrean history.

Moreover, during my interaction with student as well as natives, I realized that they were grossly ignorant of ancient Eritrean past. They also misinterpreted Aksum civilization as the sole heritage of Ethiopia. Interestingly despite of all these the facts, Eritrean history is being taught comprehensively to First Degree (B.A Honours) history student and others in CASS. It also forms substantial part of the syllabus of Horn of Africa in various universities across the world.

Besides all these, the researches into the origin and evolution of complex societies and the recent developments in archaeological exploration, excavation, and interpretation in Eritrea have raised new and important questions about how its history and archaeology has been written and represented particularly the ancient phase.

All these inspired me to conduct researches and write a comprehensive book on ancient and medieval history of Eritrea. Consequently, a broad plan was made. The first task was to collect as much data as possible from archives, libraries, and field works. It consumed several years. But frustrating moment also came on the way of this project especially due to bureaucratic red tapism. However, I was able to maintain my enthusiasm and sense of a mission throughout. Once data collection was finished, I classified, explored, analyzed, and interpreted them. Thereafter, I penned them down.

All these processes took five years and finally the present work saw the light of the day.

This book is divided into twelve chapters besides a useful bibliography. Each chapter starts with an introduction followed by a discussion on the main theme (under headings and sub-headings) and then ends up with a conclusion. Wherever needed and possible suitable map, table, and photo have been provided for better understanding of the subject matter.

The first chapter "Historiography" dwells upon major ideological and historiographical trends in African and Eritrean history. It delineates the type of historians working on African history. Then it moves on to explore and analyze the way and kind of historical researches and writings on Africa and Eritrea in the past and prospects in future. The pre-colonial and colonial African historiographies have also been examined. It also reflects on how African and Eritrean history should be taught to the students.

"Archaeology in Eritrea" constitutes the second chapter. As the title suggests, it gives an overview of archaeological potential, researches, and activities in Eritrea. The chapter highlights the institutions playing important role in this field. It also comes up with certain suggestions and recommendations for better state of affairs for archaeology in the country.

The third chapter "Ecological Setting" gives a glimpse of Eritrean topography, climate, vegetation, flora, and fauna. It also probes into the evolution of present name Eritrea. An attempt has been made to see the correlation between its geography and historical developments.

The fourth chapter "The People" explores the historical root and evolution of Eritrean population. Generally, the present inhabitants of Eritrea have been divided into three linguistic and nine ethnic groups. An account of each of them including their settlement and subsistence patterns has been provided. The chapter also explores the similarities and dissimilarities among them.

"Prehistory" forms the fifth chapter of the present work. It deals with the prehistoric developments in Africa in general (especially human evolution) and Eritrean context in particular. The discussion begins with tracing out the possible routes of dispersal of human's ancestors from Africa to other parts of the world with special reference to Eritrea. Then it examines the developments during Paleolithic, Mesolithic, and Neolithic periods in Eritrea.

The sixth chapter "Rock Art" as the name suggests provides the survey and analysis of rock art in Eritrea. First of all, it shows the physical distribution and important centers of rock art in the country. Then it examines the setting, style, content, significance, and meaning of Eritrean rock arts.

The seventh chapter "Pre and Proto-Aksumite Era" deals with historical developments in Eritrea before and during the early phase of Aksum civilization. The material and socio-cultural milieu of the contemporary communities have been discussed.

"Ona Culture" constitutes the eighth chapter. It investigates into the ancient Ona communities whose evidences have been found in Asmara and neighbouring areas. Their political, economic, and socio-cultural lives have been examined besides settlement pattern and urban structure. A discussion on its significance for the history of Eritrea and Horn has also been provided.

The ninth chapter "Adulite Era" explains Adulis port city and its enormous influence in the region during ancient period. The chapter begins with a discussion on etymology and sources available for its historical reconstruction. Further, the political aspect and affiliation, socio-economic life, and ups and down have been analyzed.

The tenth chapter "Aksumite Period" deals with the historical developments in Eritrea during the phase of great Aksumite civilization. It tries to reconstruct Eritrean contribution to this famous ancient civilization. The chapter throws light on several Aksumite period settlements and remains especially in southern part of Eritrea and their association with overall Aksumite political, economic, and social milieus. An attempt has been made to remove the common misconception about Aksumite civilization being the so called exclusive heritage of Ethiopians.

It is followed by a chapter on "Post-Aksumite Period" dealing with the history of Eritrea between 8th-13th centuries. It explores and analyzes the three important historical developments in the region (Bejas, population migration, and Islamic expansion) during this period. First of all, a discussion on the origin, establishment, rise, and expansion of Bejas has been given. Then the chapter traces out the vast population migration in Eritrea during this phase. Finally, Islamic expansion in this region has been explained.

The twelfth and the last chapter "Heritage Management" discusses the present state, prospects, and challenges related to management of historical and archaeological heritages in Eritrea. First of all, it highlights the heritage potential of this country followed by a discussion on heritage governance and challenges. Later the heritage and site management aspects have been discussed. Towards the end, the author also forwards certain suggestion and recommendation for preservation and management of the vast and invaluable heritage resources in Eritrea and its possible uses for the socio-economic upliftment of the local communities.

This scientific investigation and interpretation of the ancient Eritrean history and archaeology would definitely liberate Eritreans and world from its gross historical misconceptions and point to unambiguous roots in the distant past. It might also help in giving confidence and strengthening the national identity and consciousness to the Eritreans. As we know that the right practice of history and archaeology can play key role in constructing the identity among people.

The use of 'he' instead of 'she' at several places is just for the sake of convenience. Any suggestion, comment, and criticism which may help in improving the book in future are welcome. The author can be reached at ramankumarsoni@gmail.com. So, I hope and wish that this book will go to long way in quenching the curiosity of masses as well as the student and teachers in classrooms.

I would be grateful to give my regards to those people who gave their valuable time, energy, and precious wishes. First of all, I would like to thank the staff members of Asmara University Library (especially Seniat) and Research and Documentation Center (RDC), Asmara (particularly Tesfalem) without whose help it would have been extremely difficult to complete the present work. I would also thank the staff members of Asmara Public Library, British Council, and EIT Library.

I am deeply obliged to Nguse Berhe, Anto A. Paul, and Dr. Krishna Rao for stimulating and motivating me to work on Eritrean history and archaeology. I am very thankful to my former Head of Department, Dr. T. Vijay Kumar who gave me enough opportunity to teach African history. It went a long way in shaping my ideas and views on the present subject matter. I owe special thanks to my friends Dr. Teena, Ajeep, and Akhilesh Kumar for helping me in editing this work.

Thanks also goes to Dr. Ogbaghebriel Berakhi, Late Tekeste Melake, Habtai Zerai, Dr. Woldetinsae Towelde, Dr. Berhane Keletu, Rezene, Kesete Teweldebrahan, Asmelash Aymut, Michael, Habtom, Aron Andemichael, Biyan, Nebsarat, Eikalu, Samuel, Miriam, Dr. Firdos Anwar, Dr. Aruna Sharma, Late Dr. J. P. Sharma, Dr. R. C. Thakran, Dr. Amar Singh, Late Dr. Surajvan, Dr. R. C. P. Yadav, Dr. Suresh Chaudhary, Dr. R. K. K. Rajrajan, Dr. N. K. Pandey, Dr. P. K. Mohanty, Dr. B. P. Shau, Dr. Tribhuvan Prasad, Dr. K. Krishna Rao, Dr. S. C. Mishra, Dr. Imtiaz Ahmad, Dr. D. N. Jha, Dr. Verma, Dr. M. V. Krishnappa, Dr. Ravindra Bhardwaj, Prof. Rajiv Dubey,

Dr. Qamar Hasan, Dr. Ganesh Prasad, Dr. Nagendra Kumar, Dr. K. P. Yadav, Ravish Nagpal, Anil Kumar Singh, Mukesh, Prabhat Kumar, Kumar Amrendar Singh, Sabbir Ahmad, Bachneshwar Paswan, Inder Chandra Bothra, for their help, encouragement, advice, and precious time.

I extend heartfelt thanks to my friends Dr. Mohammad Ehrar Alam, Ashutosh, Shiv Shankar, Ajay, Jaybardhan, Brajesh, Rakesh, Mahinder, Asif, Madan, Manoj, Dr. Mansoor, Dr. Saleem, Dr. Minhazul, Dr. Afsar Alam, Dr. Zubair, Dr. Neeraj, Dr. Garnayak, Dr. Sanober, Vipan Kumar, Ajit, Yoges Babu, Sudhakar, Sujeet, Kishore, Amit, Saroj, Sunil, Jay Prakash, Mithilesh Ranjan, Hemant, Shivani, Anil, Rani, Preeti, and Doli for their kind help and encouragement. I am also indebted to Rakesh Goyal and Kaveri Book Service for bringing this work in public domain.

Lastly, I owe thanks to my family members for their immense love and support. In fact, wife Gunjan is instrumental in motivating me to finish this work. My father and mother have always been source of inspiration for me. They are my role models. The loving hand of my dear brother and sister-in-law and the fond memories of Harshita, Aditya, and Anjali while being far away from home kept me going.

Dr. Raman Kumar Soni

List of Maps

List of Tables

List of Figures

Chapter 7: Pre and Proto-Aksumite Era

Chapter 8: Ona Culture

Chapter 10: Aksumite Period

1

Historiography

For a long time, all kinds of myths and prejudices have been concealing the true history of Africa and Eritrea from the world at large. African societies in general and Eritrean in particular were looked upon as societies that could have no history. In spite of important work done by Leo Frobenius, Maurice Delafosse, Arturo Labriola, *Stuart* Munro-Hay, Francis Anfray, Rudolfo Fattovich, Othman Saleh Sabby, Woldeab Woldemariam, Stephen H. Longrigg, Greenfield Richard, Peter R. Schmidt, Matthew C. Curtis, and Zelalem Teka; a great many non-African and non-Eritrean experts could not rid themselves of certain pre-conceptions. They argued that the lack of written sources and documents made it impossible to engage in any scientific study of these societies.

TYPES OF HISTORIAN ON AFRICA

There are two types of historians on Africa: Africanist historian and African historian. Africanist historians are those historians who are not a native African, but are working on African history. They have emerged primarily outside of the Africa. Until recently, the great majority of these historians were not Africans. They did not belong to the societies whose history was written. African history for them is a scholarly discipline, a field of thought, and a profession practiced. Africanist tradition is based on a classical scholarly tradition that utilizes the organization of colloquia and seminars as means of action. Africanist can also change their field and even can retool them and immerse in another reality entirely. It was assumed that Africanist historian had the advantage over their African colleagues in not confusing mythical time with scientific time.

It is believed that there could be no true flowering of African history as long as there are no African historians. For African historian, African history is not just a research and teaching field, but rather they have to live it and put up with the consequences and setback of this history. They do not have the privilege of mobility like Africanist historian. Once a class of educated Africans emerged, the first task that fell to them was that of correcting what had already been said and written by Africanist historians such as to re-establish the truth, to de-falsify what had already been done, and to point out the mistakes that had been committed.

Another African historian adopts a double role as an observer and actor. They are expected to maintain a sense of proportion. The African historian also views the real problem differently from what the Africanist historian views it. But they remain dependent on theories of western origin. They are still consumer of ideas developed elsewhere and exporter of the field data needed in European, American, and Asian universities to establish scholarly syntheses. Africans with western derived university training have accepted the European conception and techniques of historical investigation even though they do question some specific occidental conceptions of Africa.

THE PAST HISTORICAL RESEARCHES AND WRITINGS

With only a few rare exceptions, missionaries and administrators preceded the scholars into the field and thus established the foundations for our vision of Africa as well as Eritrea. But they pursue their own well defined objectives. Moreover, their perceptions were often moulded by predetermined aim and goal.[1] Our present perceptions of Africa and Eritrea; and understanding of their past are conditioned by the epistemological categories[2] well established in last few centuries and in large part derived from the observations of administrators, missionaries, and various travellers. Their perceptions were translated directly and uncritically into their conclusions and, which once published have often been accepted as fact.

Three visions have dominated research for more than a century such as the Biblical vision, the racist or colonial vision, and the biological[3] vision. All are tied to the dominant tendencies of the western thought. Moreover, the social reality of Africa and Eritrea continues to be described in terms of tribe and clan and reflected in the mirror of savage. The principles of interpretation of the African past and the images of this continent have varied over time. But often these changes in perception result less from the accumulation of new data or new analytic techniques than from social changes within European societies.

Very few historians have systematically examined the relation of the ethnographic questionnaires and their by-product.[4] According to western notion, civilization means the domestication of agriculture and animal husbandry, urbanization, the accumulation of wealth and its sponsorship of art, music and architecture, the skill of writing and the cultivation, learning and the pursuit of scientific knowledge built on the recorded discoveries of the past. But according to westerns, Africans rarely had wheel. They did not have the plough. Africans built their dwellings only in mud and straw. The stone buildings at Zimbabwe were passed off as relics of some long forgotten foreign civilization. They had crafts but not arts. They did not write, so discoveries could not be recorded and scientific progress could only be slowest. Their wealth was barely exploited by the Africans themselves. So, Africans and Eritrean were not civilized according to the aforesaid definitions of civilizations.

There was refusal to see Africans and Eritreans as the creator of original cultures which flowered and survived over the centuries in patterns of their own making. The continent of Africa was hardly ever looked upon as a historical entity. They believed that a split had existed from time immemorial, between a white Africa and a black Africa, each unaware of the others' existence. The Sahara was often presented as an impenetrable space preventing any intermingling of ethnic groups and peoples or any exchange of goods, beliefs, customs, and ideas between the societies that had grown upon either side of the desert. Hermetic frontiers were drawn between the civilizations of Ancient Egypt and Nubia and those of the peoples south of the Sahara.

In fact, Africans were not organized for civilization and it was Europeans who had done it for them. African past by contrast was nothing more than the unrewarding gyrations of barbarous tribes in picturesque but irrelevant corners of the globe. Some western Africanist historian argued that perhaps in the future, there will be some African history, but at present there is none. There is only the history of the Europeans in Africa.

The phenomenon which did great disservice to the objective study of the African past was the slave trade, colonization, and racial stereotypes which bred contempt and lack of understanding. It became so deep-rooted that these distorted even the basic concepts of historiography. Africans were identifiable by the colour of their skin. They had become a kind of merchandise. Africans were earmarked for hard labour and came to symbolize an imaginary and allegedly 'inferior Negro race.' This pattern of spurious identification relegated the history of the African people in many minds to the rank of ethno-history, in which appreciation of the historical and cultural facts was bound to be warped. In fact, the colonized Africans had to struggle against both economic and psychological enslavement.

African and Eritrean oral tradition[5] has been rejected as worthless. The sources used were mainly from outside the continent, and the final product gave a picture not so much of the paths actually taken by the African peoples. The modes of production, social relations, and political institutions were visualized only by reference to the European past.

An eminent Africanist, 'after having noted the existence of African history,' concludes on a fairly pessimistic note. He writes that African history is like a cloth, where there are more holes than cloth, thus evoking the lack of written documents on African history. African researchers very often had a tendency to examine only those subjects for which there exist abundant sources. For instance, one finds abundant work on the colonial and post-colonial history of Eritrea. Thus African and Eritrean history often has been written from the point of view of the existing sources and not from the perspective of the problems that relate to the question of African and Eritrean consciousness.

PRE-COLONIAL AFRICAN HISTORIOGRAPHY

It would be interesting to study and conduct research on pre-colonial history. This is the period, when Africa and Eritrea was still the master of its own destiny. It is a period for which reflection on the capacities of the historical initiatives of African and Eritrean people can be applied most usefully outside the colonialist control over theoretical suppositions. The study of pre-colonial Africa and Eritrea, based on anthropological work, presupposes the establishment of scientific concepts and categories. It is also a period of African and Eritrean history for which the mobilization of the essential sources of its own culture is most imperative. Oral traditions are not sufficient for these purposes. Other methods must also be found along with the exploration and development of other forms of analysis. It is in this field that the effort of reflection on and conceptualization of history demands greater originality and creativity. This is because new explanatory theories must be constructed.

Moreover, while dealing with the pre-colonial period, it is necessary to seize the specific idiom[6] through which the historical consciousness of African and Eritrean people is expressed such as the meaning of myths, legend and symbols; and the meaning of institutions and of customs.[7] The comprehension of forms and content of traditional history must allow the establishment of epistemological bases for an objective reconstruction and interpretation of the facts. Born in the wake of ethnography, the historiography of the pre-colonial period has long been a micro-history of ethnic group, which privileged the description of migrations of institutions and customs at the expense of any full understanding of historical dynamics.

Bringing the concepts of mode of production, culture, ideology, social formation and articulation permits the most daring historians to throw new light on the historical evolution of pre-colonial African and Eritrean societies. This type of history allows for greater clarity on problems of the present. The vision of world history form Africa is the vision of history from the perspective of the real problems in Africa.

COLONIAL AFRICAN HISTORIOGRAPHY

In the past four or so decades, the focus of research has been on the nationalist struggle, the leadership, platform and organization of political parties, and the form of government with which each nation embarked on independence. In the selection of material and in the differing emphasis placed upon events, nationalism and the evolutionist ideas behind it dominated the writing of African and Eritrean history from independence onwards. This produced three main kinds of distortions.

First, a historicism was introduced, assigning various communities to stages of development, thus obscuring their role in their own time and place. Second, the subject was narrowed to the evolutionary areas. Where historians found evidence of forms of organization which resembled those of the European past, they extrapolated the form of evolutionary trends, treating the rest as peripheral history. Third, values were allowed very much to dictate what could appear in the new history books and how it would be represented.

But in succeeding period, African history moved from a position of supporting new elites to embracing the poor of Africa. Historians working on Africa adopted two approaches such as nationalist and Marxist. But, both models are western ones. Western Africanist historians go into the study of Africa with certain principled expectations of Africans derived from their views of western history. The African historians who emerged in the erstwhile African colonies offered the new nations an anti-colonial history paying the new leadership the compliment of identifying its interests with that of the country as a whole.

There are several paradigms on the colonial historiography. Some of these paradigms are the Commonwealth Tradition, the Political Economy Framework, the British World System Approach, and the Romantic Nationalist Paradigm etc.

The Commonwealth Paradigm was built around the British custom of devolving power peacefully to former colonies during the nineteenth and early twentieth centuries. Several historians stress the prime importance of the commonwealth tradition of devolution of power from London leading to African decolonization. Some scholars have argued that African decolonization was planned from within the British government shortly after the World War II. The principal arguments in this approach are over personalities and timing. Flint has suggested that planning for African decolonization within the colonial office effectively began even before World War II. R. Robinsons further suggest that strategy for post-war reconstruction in Britain's African colonies through staged devolution of power and economic development was enormously and unexpectedly speeded up by certain riots in African colonies.

But the question arise, as why those groups who became so active do so, while others no less oppressed, remain less involved. According to R. Rathmore, it was an emergent petty bourgeoisie which constituted the core and backbone of anti-colonial nationalism.

It was because of the fact that they bore the brunt of colonial restriction, shared few of the limited privileges brought by colonialism, and through their limited literacy and location in modern occupational strata were most likely to be receptive to the sophisticated ideological and organizational creations of nationalist leaders.

It was composed of an entirely new generation of aspirants, no different in many respects from their counterparts in the national parties, and a new generation of businessmen which found support for these kinds of parties as their only means of entering the gainful sectors of the economy. Rathmore further argues that in the terminal colonial period, the rapidity of change especially in the social and political arena was the repercussions of a boom economy. So powerful were these transformations that they led not only to fierce economic competition but also to a real struggle for political power. He also asserts the referee function of both the British government and the public opinion.

The Political Economy Paradigm analyzes the question of "Independence for whom?" in terms of demands for freedom from colonial rule. Its protagonists say that independence from master country did not benefit all colonial people equally. They resisted the idea that there were classes and class struggles in Africa. Its supporter focuses upon the successive stages by which colony was incorporated into the expanding world capitalist economy during the period of formal empire and how certain social strata were brought into existence which in turn presence would ultimately make direct rule by the metropolitan power unnecessary. The national petty bourgeoisie also evolved in colonies.

Once having sensed the initial stirrings of discontent, the colonial government characteristically began to evolve a strategy of decolonization on the basis of which it began to bargain with an African group eager to agree to marriages of convenience all along the line. The resultant successor state, as F. Fanon and J. Saul stressed, could represent merely a change in the colour of those in positions of authority, while maintaining its internal socio-economic structure and major links with the outside world more or less intact.

According to R. Buijtenuijs, J. Lonsdale, and D. Throup recent researches present a complex picture of disparate social movements in erstwhile colonies, sometimes overlapping one another, at other times going off in different directions such as squatters revolt, resistance against enforced agricultural improvement schemes, a cultural revival, an internal civil war, and a anti-colonial movement echoing earlier primary resistance against the initial imposition of colonial rule. According to A. G. Hopkins, opposition to colonialism was based on an imperfect alliance of three major interest groups of farmer, traders, and wage-earners all of whom shared a degree of commitment to the exchange economy which distinguished them from the bulk of the population.

But, this argument is disdainful of politics and side steps the crucial question as why opposition to colonialism by such disparate interests took the form of radical nationalist sentiment? In fact, Hopkins and most other proponents of the political economy approach are surely wrong in treating African anti-colonialism as simplistically reducible to economic interest without reference to political context. The Political Economy Paradigm has been strengthened by the mushrooming of southern African studies around scholars like Shula Marks and Stanley Trapido. But until recently, these scholars have been more concerned with initial colonization rather than decolonization.

As far as the British World System Paradigm is concerned, Robinson believes that at every stage from external imperialism to decolonization, the working of imperialism was determined by the indigenous collaborative systems connecting its European and Afro-Asian components. When the colonial rulers had run out of indigenous collaborators, they either had to choose to leave or were compelled to go. In fact, the inversion of collaboration into non-cooperation largely determined the timing of decolonization. Robinson further argued that the attempts to democratize colonial governments gradually from below, swiftly manufactured popular national movements. R. F. Holland said that it was African nationalists much more than colonial authorities, who feared populist disturbances, since such an out-spilling of politics would reveal their own organizations as the ramshackle affairs, they so frequently were. Darwin stresses that nothing stimulated political mobilization in the British colonies more than London's efforts to encourage economic development.

British policy on decolonization is also understood in terms of either justificatory rhetoric regarding the importance of individual British cabinet ministers in decision making, or as a desperate quest by the British power elite to retain whatever world power was possible through NATO, the nuclear deterrent, and informal influence; now that formal empire again seemed on the way out. J. Gallagher in his Ford lectures argued that in West Africa, mass parties were the sum of a series of local political situations converted by government machinery into the apparent expression of nationalist demands. Government needed economic growth and that would have to be paid for by political concession. He further suggests that there were no freedom fighters in West Africa as there was nothing to fight over except time table. If, they were in East and Central Africa then it was white settlers. J. Hargreaves asserts that nationalist crises on the African continent were held largely responsible for bringing imperialists into Africa. Gallagher assigns them a lesser role in accelerating the end of empire.

The Nationalist Romantic Paradigm was developed in 1960s. Hopkins, one of its proponent argued that African nationalism was a spontaneous, mass movement of the downtrodden, directed against exploiting masters and led by men whose readiness for self-sacrifice was matched only by their determination to survive long enough to improve the living standards of their fellow countrymen. But this paradigm is no longer accepted.

First of all, there does not seem to have been a spontaneous and mass movement of the downtrodden. This is lucid from the studies made by Davidson and more recently Iliffe. T. Hodgkin was another pioneer of African Nationalist historiography. He emphasized on policies of the colonial powers. But, the post-Fanon fashion within the romantic nationalist paradigm treat the more violent kinds of nationalist movement as morally superior to earlier consensual decolonization attempts regardless of crucial differences. As G. Shepperson remarked that all nationalism in Africa is the product of a reaction against external forces.

Subsequently, historical study of African nationalism particularly in East and Central Africa concentrated upon the African side of this story, stressing the origins of nationalism and proto-nationalism, debating the comparative importance of elite leadership and mass support and the connections between primary resistance movements in the early colonial period and later political parties. But subsequent scholars disillusioned on discovering that many nationalist leaders had not behaved as their earlier rhetoric promised. In fact, when the first nationalist leaders of independent African countries were overthrown by military coups in the 1960s and 1970s, armies seemed to be a more crucial political institutions rather than political parties itself for studies.

ERITREAN HISTORIOGRAPHY

No people have a unique claim to history. Every people and every nation has history. Unfortunately, the past of nation under colonial domination has remained largely unrepresented. Eritrea is no exception to this. Much of Eritrea's history has not been recorded. This is especially true of its remote past or ancient history.

With the passing of Ethiopia's emperors and the decay of empire we are losing the emperor's chroniclers. In fact, foreign propagandists and even scholars served the imperial purpose. The result has been that the history of the Horn of Africa has tended to be portrayed as a history of one set of kings and their courtiers and bishops, rather than of whole people.

The centers of nationalism other than at the then current imperial centre of the Abyssinian Empire have been neglected. The writings of those who could not see their way to subscribe to such doctrines as the 'divine right of kings' were omitted from bibliographies and even castigated in that absence. However, the so called ephemeral writings of Eritrean and others and the work of a number of serious foreign journalists are very useful. Moreover, a critical re-reading can on occasion prove revealing both in what is included and perhaps misinterpreted and what is denied. A great task to re-examine and reassess all the sources lies before all of us.

There is a wider lack of precision in the use of terminology especially the ones inherited from colonial studies. For instance take the terms of 'nation' and 'tribe'. Historians have failed to recognize the Kikuyu and the Zulu as nations. It leads to the theory or more properly the assumption that all nationalism in Africa and therefore nations in Africa have grown completely out of recent colonial experience. Such an argument is basically ethnic.

THE FUTURE RESEARCHES AND HISTORICAL WRITINGS

In terms of research, a scientific and objective analysis of the African and Eritrean past based on all the sources provided by both traditional cultures and universal historiography should be made. The establishment of a scientific history has thus become a necessity for the contemporary Africa and Eritrea because the construction of new nations demands a new approach to history at a more general level. With the diffusion of writing and modern instruction, history becomes the concern of peoples and nations. African nations need to develop a collective psyche by the entrenchment of their consciousness in the organic past of the peoples.

African and Eritrean history must therefore become positive, critical, and relevant by the establishment of demythologized facts; and with the application of both internal and external critique to documents derived from oral tradition, to pre-colonial texts and colonial archives. Then they will be able to distance itself from ideological history in the Marxist sense of mystification or of auto-mystification, of codified illusions or of speculative chimeras,[8] and base its discourse on real knowledge.

There should be a new and careful study of both the areas of historiography and cultural identity. There is historical unity of Africa. Africa also enjoyed relations with the other continents such as Asia, Europe, Americas, and the Caribbean. The history clearly shows Africa's relations with southern Asia across the Indian Ocean and the African contributions to the other civilizations through mutual exchanges. For a long time, the creative manifestations of the descendants of Africans in the Americas were lumped together by some historians as heterogeneous collection of Africanisms.

Sources are very important for the construction of any history.[9] As far as the sources for African and Eritrean history is concerned, the first among them is archaeology, which holds many of the keys to the history of its cultures and civilizations. But, another very important source is oral tradition that emerged as an invaluable instrument for discovering the history of Africa and Eritrea. It makes us understand the African vision of the world from the inside and to grasp the original features of the values on which the cultures and institutions of the continent are based.

In case of Eritrea, the archaeological sources, literary sources, oral traditions, and foreign accounts are very vital. Archaeological sources hold special promise in this regard. Its study is quite indispensable to fill gaps in Eritrean history. Eritrea is incredibly endowed with the surviving traces of most precious inheritance of human achievements. Eritrean archaeological sites hold a rich and unparalleled cultural heritage covering practically all segments of the human history. A lot of invaluable archaeological sites have been identified in the country while many more potential but equally important sites are expected to be uncovered in the course of time.

There are various essential issues in African history to be focused upon. It includes the study of slave trade; colonization, with all the effects it had on population, economies, psychology and culture; relations between Africa south of the Sahara and the Arab world; and finally the process of decolonization and nation-building which mobilized the intelligence and passion of people still alive and active today.

As far as Eritrean history is concerned, there is immediate need to focus on its ancient past. The researcher should explore Eritrean geographical features and ecological settings since antiquity and analyze their influence upon its historical experiences. The prehistoric study could shed some light on early coastal adaptations in Horn of Africa; origin and dispersal of modern humans; and the possibilities of Horn being a launching point for circum-Indian Ocean dispersal etc. (Kingdon 1993; Stringer 2002). The other important area of research could be its rich and diverse rock art.

Recently, the "Pre-Aksumite" and "Proto-Aksumite" cultural studies have gathered momentum. The "Pre-Aksumite" Ona sites have assisted in breaking some of the previously held myths.[10] The archaeological findings from these sites would help in verifying the local historical sources too. The archaeological research on these Ona sites would go a long way in building historical national identity of Eritrea. This has special significance as Eritrea does not have a long and deep written history. The archaeological data from these sites also possess immense scientific value. These data can assist in making some important generalization about the past. They could help us in understanding the life cycle[11] of the early agro-pastoral communities.

A systematic and scientific study of "Pre-Aksumite" and Aksumite sites like Adulis could help us in understanding its role in the rise and fall of contiguous city-states and kingdoms.[12] Adulis bore national as well as international significance. Similarly, Qohaito is considered to be a vital gateway to the "ancient world" in the Horn of Africa. It could help us in unravelling the productive capacity of this part of ancient Eritrea. It might also prove to be important historical evidence in understanding the ancient complex society in this part of the world. There is urgent need for comprehensive survey in Qohaito, preparation of archaeological inventory, excavation of representative sites, and their management plan.[13] Qohaito has remained silent till now. There is need to open it in order to bring greater clarity to one of the most important period of human history in northern Horn. It is also suitable for carrying research on 'non-elite' human communities of the past.

The "Pre-Aksumite" and "Proto-Aksumite" site like Keskese has the potential to provide insights into inter-regional interaction in the northern Horn, including ideas about south Arabian influence on the development of "Pre-Aksumite" culture and the possible roles and functions of ritual activity during the 1st millennium BCE. Ham exemplifies the diversity represented in the Classical Age archaeological sites of Akkele Guzai. (Curtis and Habtemichael 2008).

There are number of questions to be answered through future researches. How Matara was linked to or separated from the Aksumite polity and imperial system? What roles did sites such as Keskese and Addi Gramaten play in the creation of symbolic systems and regional identities during the "Pre-Aksumite" period? What Akkele Guzai region could tell us about relationships between highland communities in the south with those in the adjacent Hamasien region and the Ona culture area of the Greater Asmara? (Curtis and Habtemichael 2008). The Akkele Guzai region is crucial for our understanding of developments that gave rise to complex societies in the northern Horn of Africa during the 1st millennium BCE and the growth of political, economic, and social structures associated with state expansion in the 1st millennium CE. The "Post-Aksumite" Eritrean history was dominated by such important phenomena as the rule of great Bejas, unprecedented population migration, and the expansion of Islam. There are urgent needs for a sincere study in all these issues.

Today, as formerly, Africa aspires to a unified consciousness. But this theme can play negative as well as positive role. It plays negative role, if it implies a unified conscience in the old style. On the other hand, it plays positive role, if it presupposes the recognition of divisions, the scientific analysis of these divisions, of their consequences for the society, and the ways and means of the abolition of division.

In this way, the new history will be able to contribute to the development of consciousness at both the national and African levels, to the affirmation of the spirit of responsibility, and to the formation of African citizens conscious of their place and of role in today's society as citizens through solidarity with all the people of the world, who are undergoing the same necessities and in turn influenced by the same realities.

THE TEACHING OF AFRICAN AND ERITREAN HISTORY

As far teaching of African and Eritrean history is concerned, one should teach historical reflection. The discovery of the African and Eritrean past must enable the student to penetrate its socio-cultural milieu, to develop reflection by the consideration of evidence of larger unities in the reconstruction of events, and search for the most pertinent articulations (something connecting different parts) between historical periods. The development of historical reflection requires also the restitution to African and Eritrean history of its fundamental intelligibility.

In fact, African studies are currently going through a period of fundamental reassessment. The Africanist historian and the African Historian fully share neither the same responsibilities nor the same existential constraints. In some respects, African academics are closer to their colleagues in western universities than to the peasants of their own nation. There is a difference between those who practice Africanism only as a professional career and those who live out the present history of Africa.

But, the two different conceptions, Africanist and African could not persist for very long without developing a third, more conciliatory and in fact more realistic approach. In fact, the supposed barriers between them were not so formidable. Their characteristics can be shared between them. The Africanist should try to document the African and Eritrean history[14] still buried in European and American archival depositories and private collections. They should also provide properly annotated translations of certain texts. There are need for an African concept of history, which would provide for the reassessment of the facts of African and World history from the African perspective.

Sources of African origin are best exploited by African historians. The corpus of oral traditions must be established by them and published with the necessary annotations[15] so that they may be equally intelligible to specialists situated abroad who may be drawn to use them. Local archives[16] must also be made the object of systematic exploitation. The visions of the past will remain subjective even in future, but the subjectivity itself can become more likely to the mind of the reader. Therefore, research must proceed to a global reconstruction of African history, that is to a study of all periods and all peoples without exception, so that the history of Africa and Eritrea will no longer be only the history of kingdoms and empires of the past, or to the formation of colonial territories alone.

We must get away from existing paradigms because they have become too effective at encapsulating our thought.[17] We can pursue a more dialectic form of inquiry. There is need of a new historiographical paradigm within which the complexities of African nationalism and the dialectical relationships over time between the various constituent elements of these nationalist movements among themselves and with their respective colonial rulers may be studied. In the present economic circumstances, it seems highly unlikely that the local intricacies of anti-colonial nationalism in the terminal colonial period will be intensively studied by African historians themselves and hence the disparagement of anti-colonial movements is likely to remain unchallenged from within Africa. We need to develop greater understanding of the regional base for party loyalties involving the interplay between social groups[18] defined in material terms[19] and the realms of ideology and consciousness.

As far as Eritrean history is concerned, there is a need to write an alternative history by eliminating political justifications and myths of colonial researchers and writers. Now, some of the young and dedicated cadre of Eritrean archaeologists, historians, and researchers are attempting to reconstruct its history. The role of institutions like Eritrean National Museum assumes enormous importance in the given circumstances and desired endeavour. The Museum is manned with well trained and highly devoted specialists and professionals. In fact, it seems to be spearheading the initiative.

ENDNOTES

1. The administration sought the former structures on which to build the colonial order. The thumb rule was to maintain the local institutions even while abolishing the customs considered contrary to public order.
2. It refers to theories, foundations, and scope.
3. It is also known as technological vision.
4. It means the ethnographic monograph.
5. The oral tradition refers to the collective memory of peoples which holds the thread of many events marking their lives.
6. These idioms should be naturally native.
7. But above all the meaning of the type of discourse that formalizes them and makes them explicit.
8. It refers to an imaginary monster

9. The types of sources have a very significant role to play in the reconstruction of any history.
10. One of the important and widely believed myths is the development of sedentary communities in Eritrea from south Arabia.
11. This life cycle includes rise, location, nature, and decline of these communities.
12. The kingdom here refers to Aksum and Meroe.
13. The archaeological sites on the Qohaito and Adikeih Plateaus are under constant threat due to expansion of housing and agricultural development and rock quarrying activities. (Schmidt, et al. 2004). Rock arts have been damaged due to vandalism and the use of ancient architectural elements for local house construction.
14. According to some sources, there are hundreds of work on Eritrea preserved in the libraries and archives of Italy.
15. That means explanatory notes.
16. The Research and Documentation Center (RDC) in Asmara is one example of such local archives.
17. As within each of them there is far too little eagerness to look at alternative viewpoints with any seriousness, and far too much concern to continue along existing increasingly ramshackle line of inquiry.
18. It means ethnic and class.
19. It should include language, culture, and political power as well as relations of production.

2

Archaeology in Eritrea

The archaeology of Eritrea is a treasure house with boundless riches. It is blessed with manifold and consummate heritage resources.[1] Now, its heritage bounties have become a matter of common knowledge. According to an estimate, Eritrea possesses almost 20,000-40,000 archeological and historical sites ranging from ancient to recent time. Probably, it has the highest density of archeological sites in Africa out side the Nile valley. Some of its well-known sites are Qohaito, Matara, Keskese, Adulis, Buya, Dahlak Kebir, Nakfa, Sembel, and several other sites in Greater Asmara area. In addition to these, the monasteries of Debrie Bizen, Debre Sina Ham, and the Kidna Mehret;[2] the mosques of Sheikh Hanazi,[3] Assahaba,[4] and Sheik Hamal an Savi are archaeologically and historically very important.

SIGNIFICANCE OF ARCHAEOLOGY

Eritrea's strategic place in the development of humankind and later civilization, the diversity of its inhabitants, and mixed socio-political legacies makes it a fertile ground for cultural properties. (Habtezion 2008). It has the potential to answer several mysteries related to human history. The Danakil depression possibly holds key to some of the enigmas associated with the origins of mankind. The intensive research in Buri Peninsula and the area around Gulf of Zula may throw important light on the development of human species and its migration from Africa to other parts of the world. The area along the

Red Sea could give us some clue about the pattern of early human coastal adaptations.

The rich rock art of Eritrea might reveal its inhabitant's relationship with the contemporary communities and the role of art in their culture. Eritrea also holds promise in exploring the interchange of cultures as it is situated at the junction of three major geographical phenomena such as the Indian Ocean, the West Asia,[5] and the Africa. Furthermore, it could provide significant opportunities for study into the development of urbanism[6] and trade relation with ancient Asia,[7] Europe,[8] and Africa. Eritrea also holds lot of promise for historical archaeology. It could help historical archaeologists in understanding the development of Christianity[9] in general and some of the most ancient Christian communities in this area in particular. Eritrean archaeology may facilitate understanding Islamic history as well.[10] This great ancient land could certainly be a paradise for the ethno-archaeologist and ethno-historical experts; given its remarkable ethnic, linguistic, economic, and subsistence diversity.[11] (Schmidt and Curtis 2008).

EVOLUTION OF ARCHAEOLOGY

The archaeology in Eritrea has developed over the last one century. First of all, it was some German and Italian enthusiasts in the first half of 20th century, who brought to light the significance of Eritrean archaeology to the world. They documented some important sites such as Matara, Keskese, and Qohaito in the southern part of present Eritrea. (Littmann, et al. 1913). One Italian bank teller documented some sites in the south-western part of Asmara. (Tringali 1965, 1969). One of the greatest pioneer in Horn's archaeology,[12] Francis Anfray conducted excavation at the sites of Matara and Adulis in late 1950s, 60s, and early 70s.

There has been frantic rush of paleo-anthropologists and paleo-environmentalists in the post-independence era from across the world to the Danakil area in the hope of finding some crucial evidence of early Stone Age. A UNESCO[13] sponsored team under the leadership of Anfray visited Eritrea to assess needs of heritage legislation in 1994. It resulted into long and dense documentation. But, this failed to get the favour of incumbent government. A major breakthrough[14] was achieved with the visit of Henry Wright and Peter Schmidt[15] to Eritrea in 1995. They successfully highlighted[16] the vast potential[17] of Eritrea in the domain of archaeological research. The following year, Peter Schmidt was invited to design a curriculum in archaeology by the University of Asmara. He along with John Distefano[18] and Yosief Libseqal[19] were instrumental in designing and introducing archaeology, museum studies, and the heritage management course in the University of Asmara.

Thereafter, the Department of Archaeology was launched in 1997-98 academic year. The instructors and students of this department did a great job by moving quickly to document the sites in the Greater Asmara region and other parts of Eritrea deemed for several kind of developmental activities. Some of the sites in Greater Asmara area were found to be older than Aksumite period. It was followed by excavations at Sembel and Sembel Kushet sites.[20] This aroused immense interest among all the stakeholders such as students, general public, and power corridor[21] due to the possibility of an interesting alternative history to an Aksum dominated past of the region.

A number of students graduated with first degree in archaeology until 2001. Thereafter, the Department of Archaeology was reorganized as the Department of Anthropology and Archaeology. After sometime, this department was shifted from University of Asmara to College of Arts and Social Sciences.[22] The graduates from these departments have been deputed into several ministries,[23] agencies, and institutions as archaeological interns to assist them with cultural and historical heritage matters. At present, several Eritrean students are studying as post-graduate and Ph.D students in different universities around the world.[24] Eritrea seems to have a bright future with these young archaeologists.

NATIONAL MUSEUM

The discussion about Eritrean archaeology would remain incomplete without mentioning the pivotal role of National Museum in this area. The National Museum of Eritrea has been one of the forerunners in the field of archaeological activities; and preservation, protection, and promotion of cultural heritage in this country. Actually, it was Asmara Museum that heralded the establishment of the present National Museum of Eritrea. It was created and inaugurated in early 1992.

This museum was founded with the aim of facilitating the public view of their historical and cultural heritage that was dominated and distorted by the alien forces in the past. It also goes a long way in asserting the Eritrean historical identity. Initially, it was put under the aegis of the Ministry of Information and Culture. (Siravo 1997). Then the museum was put under the control of University of Asmara. The National Museum of Eritrea has one branch in Massawa. There are also some regional museums like the Museum of the Northern Red Sea region.

National Museum provides several facilities. It began with three sections such as the archaeology, the ethnography, and the military or war of independence. With the passage of time, it progressed to include another three sections such as paleontology, medieval, and the national history. In addition to this, it also exhibits several paintings in art gallery segment which are painted by freedom fighters. Another facility provided by it is visitor service. It incorporates a lecture room, a refreshment area, and small museum shop.

As far as Museum administration and service is concerned, it has office space for the director and deputy director and includes design, construction, and maintenance workshop, and a registry.

Museum also facilitates documentation and research activity. It includes a research library, an inventory, cataloguing and drafting room, a photographic and microfilm laboratory, a research office, and archival space. Collection and storage section includes storage area, a small handling part, and an office for accessing and recording the items in the collection, and conservation workshops for the study and preservation of artifacts in the permanent collection.

On the other hand, the museum also engages in the study, protection, and preservation of archaeological sites and antiquities. Beside this, the museum in collaboration with local and foreign institutions organizes and conducts training, exploration, excavation, restoration, public awareness programme, educational activity, and nomination of sites. Large number of domestic and foreign tourist visits National Museum as well as open air site museums annually. It also administers and enforces the law of cultural heritage protection and establishes criteria to ensure the highest scholarship and professional work standards. Moreover, Eritrean National Museum is also responsible for preserving and transferring the history of Eritrean freedom struggle.

In collaboration with the German archeological mission from Humboldt University, the National Museum conducted a survey and fencing of the Qohaito site. In addition to this, the fencing of the site of Hashmele[25] was under taken. The National Museum and an Italian paleo-anthropological research team jointly conducted a survey in the Buya area. They were successful in discovering a homo skull a million years old. Since 2001, the staff of the National Museum has carried an archaeological survey in greater Asmara region.

The museum also conducted an exploration in and around Decemhare during 2004-2005 with the help of funding from the governments of Netherland and Eritrea. In 2004, a survey of Adulis archaeological site was carried out jointly by an archaeological team consisting of members from the National Museum, University of

Asmara, and University of South Hampton. Funded by Museum and Global Resource Ltd., the museum staff members conducted an archaeological exploration in the vicinities of Dubarawa and Adi-Nefas in 2006. They also carried survey of Bisha in 2005. The museum also conducted archaeological research during Debra-Hawatsu road construction project in 2005. (Tsehaye 2008).

National Museum has also actively engaged in several excavation projects. Eritrea being a relatively young country is actively engaged in reconstruction works. So salvage excavation is a frequent phenomenon in this respect. The museum's accomplishments in this arena are commendable. Its staff member undertook a rescue excavation at Maitemenai area in 1996. It discovered a number of remarkable ceramic and metallic artifacts. In addition to this, the rescue excavation was carried at Maitchihot, Embaderho, and Sembel area. Funded by the Netherland embassy, the National Museum conducted a rescue excavation in the town of Decemhare, with in the compound of the police academy in the year 2005. So, National Museum in collaboration with the domestic and foreign originations gave effective priority for survey and rescue excavations throughout the country.

This institution has also carried restoration activities. The National Museum in collaboration with UNESCO has fully restored and erected the stele of Matara in a safe area. The ancient church of Kidane Mihret[26] was restored successfully in the year 2007. Besides that it also made several restorations of immovable heritages like rock paintings and engravings. Their supervision is facilitated by appointing guards and encircling fences.

The National Museum is also actively engaged in educational and pubic awareness activities. It delivered heritage management lesson to the site guards and religious community from various localities. This was conducted in the town of Embatcala, Mendefera, and Adikeih in the year of 1996 and 2004. Museum staffs also took care to hold meetings and discussions with the local community and its elders during the exploration and excavation work on archeological sites in Zoba Debub and Zoba Semenawi Keyh Bahri.

For instance in 1994, the museum gave lectures to the local people around Senafe. All these go a long way in the development of mutual understanding for better preservation and conservation of the precious cultural heritage. Moreover, it is also disseminating information concerning heritage issues through mass media.[27] Recently, in view of the international significance of several Eritrean heritage sites, the archeological sites of Qohaito, Dahlak, Adulis, Matara, and Nakfa have been listed for the nomination of universal heritage status. (Tsehaye 2008).

Eritrea holds great potential for understanding ancient human history. It can certainly help in inquiring the development of food production, the rise of civilization, and urbanism in this part of the world. Eritrea can contribute tremendously in the field of archaeology. But for this to happen, the government and the society should create a suitable environment for the awareness, preservation, protection and promotion of their rich cultural heritage. There should be an active and continuous coordination and cooperation between the different governmental institutions, non-government actors, academicians, and community.

The institution like the National Museum needs to be carefully nourished and strengthened. Although it is playing very important role in the domain of archaeology; and protection, preservation, and promotion of Eritrean cultural heritage, a lot more is desired. National Museum is suffering from severe shortage of funds and facilities. This great institution should be given enough autonomy to take policy decisions on heritage matters and implement it effectively and efficiently. The government of Eritrea should provide sufficient finance to the National Museum to carry extensive archaeological explorations and excavations.

It should have a large building with provision for sufficient natural light and less humidity. The institution should also consist of an appropriate lecture hall, exhibition rooms, and well equipped libraries and laboratories. Beside this, it should have its own transport facility to carry its task easily. National Museum should also try to collaborate with the public at large. All these will go a long way in the efforts to protect, preserve, and manage the valuable resources. (Gebrehiwet, et al. 2009)

The creation of an independent archaeological institution to spearhead and coordinate all the archaeological activities in the country is recommended. It could be made responsible for providing the necessary leadership in archaeological research and cultural heritage governance and management task. This central institution could have its regional and sub-regional branches in each *Zobas*[28] and districts. The institution can prepare an exhaustive inventory of national heritage through extensive and intensive archaeological explorations and excavations.

The government and other non-government institutions are expected to encourage and promote archaeological and other heritage related research through all the means at their disposal. One can also try to attract foreign funding in this regard as the cultural heritage is common to all mankind. There should be more emphasis on field archaeology. The student of archaeology needs to be given enough practical experience. There is urgent need of some specialized archaeological journals and periodicals that could provide the necessary platform for the publication of new researches made in this domain.

Government can also open a heritage management institute specializing in teaching and training programme in this area. All these institutions need to manned by highly trained and specialized professionals and technicians. We need to justify and promote archaeological education, research, and management to allow the present as well as future generation to recognize, understand, and appreciate their history and heritage. Undoubtedly, the Eritrean archaeology with all its potential has long way to go.

ENDNOTES

1. It is surprising given the relatively small area of Eritrea.
2. It is a church situated near Senafe.
3. This mosque is situated in Massawa. It is believed to be almost 500 hundred years old.
4. This mosque is located in Massawa. It was built in 615 CE.
5. Here, West Asia refers to the region for which the terminology Middle East is frequently used. But, latter may not be fully acceptable.
6. Eritrea is blessed with several ancient urban sites such as Qohaito, Matara, and Adulis etc. In their heyday, they seem to have flourished with several satellite communities.
7. It can throw significant light on trade links with Arabian Peninsula as well as India.
8. It can equally expose possible trade link between Romans and this area.
9. Eritrean cultural heritage includes extensive network of churches and monasteries belonging to 1st millennium CE.
10. It can help us in seeing the variety in Islamic history in the form of settlement in the Dahlak Archipelago to outposts in the furthest reaches of the Ottoman Empire, and Egyptian hegemony in the Red Sea.
11. Ethnicity, language, landscape, climate, and economy could be some of the interesting areas of study for ethno-archaeologist and ethno-historical experts.
12. It means the archaeology of Horn of Africa.
13. UNESCO stands for United Nations Educational, Scientific, and Cultural Organization.
14. It highlighted several aspects such as the great importance of the heritage sites in Eritrea, absence of protection for these heritages, and need of development of a training programme in archaeology and heritage management.
15. Henry Wright belonged to University of Michigan. Peter Schmidt later on joined Asmara University.

16. It was more true incase of North American audience.
17. It reflected the potential of inquiry into the development of complex societies, the development of food production, the rise of civilization and urbanism in the Horn of Africa.
18. He was the head of History Department in University of Asmara.
19. Mr. Libseqal was the interim director of National Museum at that time. Now he is the Director of this esteemed institution.
20. They are dated to the 800-400 BCE.
21. It refers to the policy makers.
22. Initially, this college was located within the premise of Eritrea Institute of Technology, Mai-Nefhi. But now it is thriving in its new campus in Adi-Keih. Latter lies in a very promising area from the point of view of historical and archaeological researches.
23. It includes the Department of Lands, the Ministry of Tourism, and several other agencies and institutions such as National Museum and CARP (Cultural Assets Rehabilitation Project) and Eritrea Institute of Technology.
24. It includes universities of western world, Japan, and Sudan etc.
25. It is around the town of Adikeih.
26. This church was built with a unique traditional architecture known as "monkeys head."
27. In response to this several people as individuals and in groups have been contacting the National Museum whenever they encounter any type of archeological artifacts. Some even come with precious artifacts. So this can be counted as one of the important achievements of the museum.
28. It refers to the provinces.

3

Ecological Setting

The geographical condition and ecological setting goes a long way in determining the history of any society or nation. This is also true of Eritrea. So, it is better to explore and analyze Eritrea's location, topography, physical features, climate, vegetation, and natural resources before moving on to reconstruct its history. Eritrea is situated along the Red Sea coast on African side, sharing a border with Sudan to the West, Ethiopia to the south and southeast, and Djibouti on its southeastern tip. It stretches roughly between 18° N latitude to 13° north latitude and 36° E longitude to 43° E longitude. Eritrea covers an area of 124300 square kilometers. It is blessed with breathtaking highland, large chunk of lowlands, and an extensive coastline flanked by coral reefs and numerous islands.

Table 1: Some basic facts about Eritrea

1.	Area	124300 square kilometers
2.	Red Sea Coastline	1151 kilometers
3.	Red Sea Islands	350
4.	Highest Point	Amba Soira, 3013 meters
5.	Lowest Point	Kobar Sink, 75 meters

NOMENCLATURE

Ancient Egyptians called the Horn of Africa of which Eritrea is a part, "Land of Punt." In 3rd century BCE, the Greeks gave the name

"Trichonesinus Erythraeum" to the seas[1] around Arabian Peninsula.[2] In the pre-Aksumite period, Eritrea and much part of Tigray were known as the kingdom of Habeshat.[3] However during the Aksumite period, it was well known as Aksumite kingdom itself. It became *"Ma'ekel Bahr"* following the decline of the Aksumites.[4] It came to be known as *"Medr-Bahr"* around 16th century. With the arrival of the Turks and their conquest of the coastal area, the name *"Mereb- Melash"* came to prevail. Finally, the territory got its present name Eritrea when the Italians occupied it in late 19th century.[5]

PHYSICAL FEATURES

The Central Plateau or Kebessa

The Central Plateau also known as Kebessa constitute the physical center of Eritrea. It is also the hub of political and economic activities. Not surprisingly, Kebessa has been center of civilization since antiquity. It receives reasonable rainfall during two rainy seasons in spring and summer (*Krimti*) to sustain cereal agriculture. The central plateau is home to more than half of the Eritrea's population. This is also where much of country's light industry is situated.

It comprises a northward pointing triangle of land averaging 2000-3000 meters in height. The eastern edge of the Kebessa is an abrupt escarpment that rises from the northern end of the East African rift valley and abuts the Denkel deserts and coastal plain in a series of steep canyons and ridges. Its northern slope, the Semenawi Bahri lands are well forested and enjoy two rainy seasons. The most important river in the area is Mareb. The western boundary of this central plateau region is less distinct. Here, it descends toward the lowlands in a maze of ravines and ridges some thirty to fifty kilometers in width.

The Northern Highlands

The northern highlands are an extension of the Kebessa, whose high plateau continues northward in a narrow band of mountains parallel to the coast all the way into Sudan. They reach 2500 meters in places, broken into many small ranges by numerous passes and river valleys. The most important river here is the Anseba. Along the river valleys and the narrow ridge tops, people have grown cereals and pastured animals for thousands of years. The strategic importance of the passes between the coast and western lowlands and the rugged redoubts of the Sahel Mountains, have made this region the site of many of Eritrea's bloodiest battles.

The Western Lowlands

The western lowlands constitute almost half of Eritrea's area. Its hills and plain averages about 800 meters in height.[6] The region receive run-off from the highlands and have rich underground water resources. While the Gash area receives substantial summer rains, the lowlands in the north are dry and thinly covered with grass and thorn bush. They can only support seasonal grazing except along the Barka River valley.

The Mareb runs out into the lowlands south of Barka, where it is called the Gash. The latter waters the rich cotton lands along the Sudanese border at Tessenei. The sedentary agriculture is possible between Barka and Gash (southwest of Agordat) as the summer rains become heavier. The Setit River flows south of the Gash in the lowland and forms Eritrea's southwestern border with Ethiopia.[7] The land is relatively rich and thickly forested in places between the Gash and the Setit. The Gash-Setit area has been populated since ancient times by Nilotic farmers. This is a region which holds high hope for modern Eritrea. It has considerable untapped agricultural potential.

The Coastal Plains

The coastal plain is a sparsely inhabited desert whose waterways are usually dry and temperatures are among the hottest in the world. The low-lying coastal areas get light winter rains and are crossed by seasonal streams during rainy season from highland plateau. Its inhabitants are mainly nomadic herders, seasonal farmers, and fishermen. The slopes along the coastal escarpment have long been the focus of intensive cropping. This area holds strong potential for future development.

The northern coastal plain averages 35 kilometers in width with sandy soils punctuated by seasonal watercourses.[8] It has few natural harbors and been historically inhabited by seasonal nomads. The central coast including Semhar province and extending south from Massawa to the Bure peninsula is more favoured. Here, the mountains almost meet the sea. It is blessed with numerous watercourses. There is a fertile plain along the western shore of the Gulf of Zula. It is watered by rivers like Alighede, Hadas, and Lomalie rivers draining the central highlands. The ports and fishing villages have been located in this region since ancient times. It has large and diverse population centered on Eritrea's principal port of Masawa. The southern coast is the most barren. It merges with the volcanic hills and alkaline wastes of Danakil together comprising the Denkel. Assab is located at its southern end.

Islands

There are more than 350 islands dotting the coastline. But most of them are concentrated in the Dahlak archipelago, east of Massawa. The largest of these, Dahlak Kebir is 643 square kilometers with a population of about 1500 in nine villages.

CLIMATE

The highest temperatures in coastal areas occur from June to August and range from 25° celcius to 40-45° celcius. But, sea breezes provide some relief, especially on the islands. The rainy season along the northern Red Sea coast comes during December-February. It is scarce along the southern Red Sea coast. In the central plateau, the highest temperatures occur in May reaching 30° celcius. However, temperatures can fall as low as the freezing point at night during winter months of December and January. The short rainy season in this area prevails during the months of April and May. The major one occurs between late June and early September.

The hottest season in the western lowlands comes in April-June with temperatures reaching 40° celcius. December is the coldest month, as temperatures drop to 10-12° celcius. But, there are dramatic temperature differences here between day and night throughout the year. The rainy season is similar to that of the plateau.

The Kebessa receives an average of 61 centimeters rainfall per year. Keren and Agrodat in the northern highlands and western lowland receive an average rainfall of 45 centimeters and 35 centimeters per year respectively. In the Denkel desert along the southern coast, rainfall drops below 10 centimeters and the temperature can rise to 50° centigrade. The temperature averages 30° in the western lowlands and 17° in the Kebessa.

VEGETATION

Flora

The eastern lowlands offer rolling acacia wood land, brush land and thicket, semi-desert vegetation, and mangrove swamp. Kassod and flame trees line the roads to many coastal towns. The central highlands are dominated by juniper and wild olive, as well as several species of acacia. East African laburnum, native hops, and eucalyptus are common along the roadsides and on steeply terraced hillsides. The Semenawi Bahri slopes north-east of Asmara are the most thickly forested in Eritrea and have remnants of dense evergreen and tropical wood-land. Southeast of Asmara, one finds majestic sycamores. The western slopes are dotted with baobab, toothbrush, and tamarisk trees. This gives way to woodland savannah, brush land, and thicket in the Barka and Gash plains, which are broken up by dense groves of doum palm along the seasonal river beds.

Fauna

Common sightings today include vervet monkeys, baboon, gazelle, jackal, hare, fox, mongoose, wild cat, squirrel, and warthog. Dikdiks and Dorcas gazelle are often seen along the coast. Less frequently observed are elephant, caracal, serval, orysx, crocodile, greater kudu, and hartebeast. The endangered wild African ass can also be found, though rarely.

Eritrea hosts an abundance of birdlife with its varied habitats. Some of them are resident round the year whereas others are seasonal. A total of 537 species have been identified, including the rare blue saw-wing. The Dahlak Islands with their rich feeding grounds attract osprey, gulls, tern, boobies, ibis, and white flamingo among many other endemic and transient species.

The moist forests of the Semenawi Bahri slopes are home to bush shrikes, francolins, sunbirds, tropical boubou, and crimson turaco, canaries, trogon, catbirds, and hornbills etc. One small lake near Asmara is frequented by blue-winged goose, Rouget's rail, and the Abyssinian long claw. Ostrich are increasingly common along the coast and in the western plains, as are African fire finches, scrub robin, and spotted sand grouse among other. Hundreds of species of the birds also migrate through Eritrea in autumn and spring.

Marine Life

Marine ecosystems include coral reefs, sea-grass beds, and mangrove forests. Patch coral extends around many of the islands. It is in rich concentration along the northern coastline. Five species of marine turtle have been identified such as green, hawksbill, leatherback, loggerhead, and ridley. Moreover, several species of dolphin are common especially around the Dahlak Islands. Whales have also been sighted.

NATURAL RESOURCES

Eritrea has rich natural resources. The mix of climates supports a wide range of crops, vegetables, and fruits. They include millet, sorghum, taff, wheat, barley, flax, cotton, coffee, papaya, citrus fruits, banana, mangos, beans, lentils, potatoes, several vegetables, fish, and dairy products.

Livestock mainly includes sheep, goat, cattle and camel. The Red Sea supports edible fish, lobster, crab, and shrimp. The coastal area has potential for intensive saltwater fishing and shrimp farming. The geological mosaic of pre-Cambrian, Mesozoic, and Cenozoic rocks holds extensive reserves of metallic, non-metallic, and fossil minerals. Potentially profitable deposits of gold, copper, zinc, potash, iron ore, and other minerals have been confirmed; while exploration continues off-shore for oil and gas. There are also significant high quality marble, granite, slate, and limestone for construction industry.

So the climatic and topographical variations have created four distinct ecological regions in Eritrea such as the coastal plain, central highland, northern highland, and western lowland. The temperate central plateau rises over two kilometers above sea level, while the scorched southeastern Danakil depression is one of the lowest dry land points on earth. To the west are the fertile lowland Barka and Gash plains. A lush green belt lies northeast of the capital city of Asmara. It also has thriving ports like Massawa and Assab.

The name Eritrea has deep ancient root. Its location and geographical setting has shaped its history to great extent. One of the best examples is its history of occupation by a succession of colonizers bent on controlling its coast. Eritrea's geographical relation to the sea gives its people their unique identity. Moreover, it enjoys very diverse demography and culture. The nation is made up of nine ethno-linguistic groups that embrace two of the world's major religions, Islam and Christianity besides indigenous minority faiths.

ENDNOTES

1. These include Red Sea, the Gulf of Aden, the Arab sea, and the Arabian Gulf.
2. They gave this name because of the reflection of a red colour out of the water surface.
3. It was during 4th century BCE to 1st century CE.
4. It took place between 11th and 14th centuries.
5. On January 1, 1890 a royal decree of Umberto I baptized the name Eritrea to the Italian oversea domain along the red sea coast.
6. Sometimes the isolated outliers of the highlands projects as much as 1500 meters.
7. It also constitutes the Ethiopian river Takezze.
8. The most important being the Felket, Lebka, and Laba.

4

The People

The nature of population is one of the important factors besides geography which plays vital role in determining the historical development of a society or region. So, it is imperative to examine the demographic composition and material milieu of Eritrean populace before embarking upon the study of its history. Eritrean population is as rich and diverse as its geography. It is inhabited by nine ethnic groups. They are mainly associated with two major language phyla of Africa such as Afro-Asiatic and Nilo-Saharan. Each of these ethnic groups has their own unique features as well as some similarity with others.

Table 2: The different ethnic groups with their approximate share in the population, language, and religion. (Killion 1998).

Ethnicity		Share in Population (%age)[1]	Language	Religion[2]
Nilotic	Nara	1%	Nara	Muslim
	Kunama	3%	Kunama	Traditional Indigenous Religion, Muslim, and Christian
Cushitic	Afar	3%	Afar	Muslim
	Bilen	5%	Bilen	Muslim and Christian
	Hedareb	-1%	To-Bedawe	Muslim
	Saho	7%	Saho	Muslim and Christian
Semitic	Tigrinya	50%	Tigrinya	Christian and Muslim
	Tigre	30%	Tigre	Muslim
	Rashaida	-1%	Arabic	Muslim

The earliest inhabitants of Eritrea and surroundings seem to have been of pygmoid type who were scattered in much of Africa, Asia, and Europe. Eritrea's population is composed of various elements received through migrations during last thousand years. Among these migrations, the most important were those of Nilotic, Kushitic, and Semitic peoples.[1] So the contemporary Eritrean population is the result of pluri-millennial processes of interaction between these three different ethnic stocks and their encounter with pre-existing strata. In course of time, those pre-existing pygmoid populace were either displaced or engrossed giving place to Nilotic people.

THE NILOTIC GROUP

The Nilotic people were one of the most ancient human groups to enter present Eritrean territory.[2] They are believed to have come from the middle of Nile[3] and entered Eritrea in different periods. These people founded an agricultural society in western Eritrean lowlands around the Gash-Setit area. The Nilotics remained there until pushed by either the Kushitic migration or the natural expansion from the Mediterranean races. Thereafter, they penetrated into Barentu plateau in search of a sanctuary.

Nowadays, the ethnic groups of Nara and Kunama[4] are considered to be their descendents. They live in western Eritrea near the borders of Sudan and Ethiopia. The Kunamas specifically live in southwestern Eritrea around the town of Barentu and are also found across the border in Ethiopia. The Nara lives in the western slopes and Barka plains. They are mostly Muslims adopting much of the Islamic culture of their Beja and Tigre neighbours. Gradually, their matrilineal family structure was transformed into a patrilineal one.

The Kunamas are mainly Christians.[5] Some of them are Muslims too. In fact, some Kunamas also follow their traditional faith, centered on worship of the creator, Anna, and veneration of ancestral heroes. Kunamas society is relatively egalitarian with distinctive matrilineal elements.

Figure 1: Author in front of a Nara Hamlet

Figure 1.1: A Kunama woman (left side).

Nara and Kunama speaks two related but different languages. Economically, both groups are agriculturalists growing sorghum, peanuts, sesame, and fruit. They farm the Gash-Setit region. Nara and Kunama have been practising slash and burn method of agriculture. They use hoe for cultivation.

THE CUSHITIC-HAMITIC GROUP

The Cushitic people were another group to enter Eritrean territory. Their origin is traced to northern Africa.[6] The several waves of migrations took place to encounter the pre-existing Nilotic people and thus giving origin to the Hamitic element. These people entered Eritrea and occupied the Barka lowlands and northern highlands. They subjugated or expelled their Nilotic inhabitants and spread along the coastal desert (lowlands of northeastern Ethiopia and the Somali land).[7]

Figure 1.2: A Hedareb hamlet.

With the passage of time, Cushitic also intermingled with Nilotic people. Currently the Afar, Bilen, Hedareb, and Saho ethnic groups of Eritrea correspond to the Cushitic people. The Cushitic languages are Afar, Bilen, Saho, and Beja. The Beja mainly Beni Amer is inhabit parts of Eritrea and Eritro-Sudanese border. They speak To-Bedawe. Beja has also largely adopted Tigre. The Hedareb are the last linguistic remnant of the great Beja-speaking population. They are also known as T'badwe and mainly inhabit a wide arc stretching from western Barka across the north-western valley of the arid and volcanic Sahel region. The Hedareb are semi-nomadic pastoralist and highly skilled camel drivers. Their Muslim society is patrilineal.

In the Senhit area of the northern highlands, the Bilen people have retained their ancient Central Cushitic language. They are found in south-central part of the country near and south to the city of Keren towards Asmara. The Bilen speak Bilin language strictly related to Agew.[8] They are mostly agriculturalist and herders and include both Muslims and Christians,[9] with former predominating. Bilen is a traditional society organized into kinship groups. Their women are known for wearing brightly coloured clothes; gold, copper or silver nose rings, and henna tattoos that resemble like diamond necklaces.

The Afar speaking people are found along the southern Red sea coast especially near Eritro-Djibouti and Eritro-Ethiopian Borders and offshore islands. They inhabit the coastal desert of Denkel area. Afar speak an Eastern Cushitic tongue. They are mostly nomadic pastoralists whose grazing extends from eastern and southern Eritrea into Ethiopia. The coastal population does include many fishermen and merchants. Some of its population also cultivates maize and tobacco near the few oases inside their territory. Traders carry slabs of salt on their camels to the highlands from the coast. The home of Eritrean Afar is the Assab region. It is a highly segmented and patrilineal society. The families live in large hemispherical houses of hides and woven mats stretched across a framework of wooden poles that can be carried by camel over long distances. They are exclusively Muslims and renowned for their prowess in battle. Afar has a long history of independent sultanates and strong warrior traditions. Their men wear the *jile* or curved knife.

Saho is a small ethnic group closely related to Afar. Their language is an Eastern Cushitic relative of Afar. Saho practices both nomadic-pastrolism and mixed farming. Some of them are seasonal farmers and herders. Still a growing number are sedentary farmers living in the southeastern highlands. Among them are skilled beekeepers. Their territory spreads from eastern Eritrea near the port of Massawa to the central Eritrean highlands as far as Hazumo valley and stretches further into Tigrai. Saho people moved into the central highland province of Akkele Guzai, where some have adopted Tigrinya culture. Saho in Eritrea are exclusively Muslim. While those in Tigrai are mostly Christians and are known are Irob. Saho lives in patrilineal descent groups, each of which has a traditional warrior leader, the *rezanto*, who is accountable to an all male public assembly.

THE SEMITIC GROUP

The Semitic people were the last group of migrants to enter Eritrean territory. They came to Eritrea between 1000-400 BCE through a series of trans-marine migrations from south Arabia.[10] They belong to Sabean people of Yemen. The main Semitic influx was around the 7th century BCE. The most important of the Semitic migration was that of the *Habashat* who migrated from the Sahartan province of Yemen. These people occupied not only Eritrea but also northern part of Tigray. Another important group was the *Ge'ez (Agazian)* who settled in the Shimezana, Akkele-Guzai, and Agame. The Semitic people intermingled with the Cushitic and transplanted their agricultural civilization in the 5th century BCE. They founded settled kingdoms in Akkele-Guzai and Seraye, which later developed into the famous kingdom of Aksum. Today the ethnic groups of Tigrinya and Tigre represent the Semitic people in Eritrea.

Even the Semitic Language family in Eritrea is represented mainly by Tigrinya and Tigre. One can also add the groups of recent

Arab origin such as Rashaida, Addi-Mualim, Addi-sheikh, and Beit Mala to this. Tigrinya speakers are mainly dominant in the highland[11] of Eritrea and Tigray with various extensions. They are principal community in the province of Serai, Hamassien, Akkele-Guzai and Tigray provinces. According to an estimate, Tigrinya is spoken by over 50% of the Eritrean population today. They are the cultural heirs of the Christian civilization that flourished in this area since 4th century CE. The majority of them belong to Coptic Orthodox Christianity. In fact, there are people who converted to Roman Catholicism and Protestantism. Jiberti Muslim is also another culturally distinct Tigrinya stock.

Tigrinya populace is sedentary agriculturalists and has maintained close cultural and economic ties with their co-linguist in Ethiopia's Tigrai province. Only 20% of them are engaged in economic activities other than agriculture. They make up a large proportion of urban traders and operators of small businesses, restaurants, and other services throughout the country. Today, the Tigrinya people make up the majority of Eritrea's internal population and dominate its political and intellectual life.

In the northern provinces of Barka and Sahel, the most important linguistic group is speakers of the Semitic tongue, Tigre. Its territory extends from the western fringes of Gash-Setit, across all of Barka and the northern highlands to the Red Sea. The Tigre speakers form the major coastal population from the Sudanese border to the Massawa area. The Tigre are divided into a number of tribes and tribal confederations, the most important being the Beni Amer, Marya, and Bet Asghede. Tigre speech is common in eastern, northern, and western Eritrea. In fact, the geographical expansion has created the differences in dialect. It is believed that the purest Tigre dialect is dominant in the region of Keren particularly among the Mensa tribes. They are closest to the Ge'ez. Apart from this, there are other groups of Tigre speech such as the Beit Juk, the Mariya

Qeih, the Mariya Tselim, the Beit Asghede, the Afflenda, the Shuma, and the Ad Asker.

Most of them are Sunni Muslim with few exceptions as Christians.[12] The majority of Tigre is agro-pastoralists, though some involved in commerce. They mainly cultivate maize, *durra* (sorghum), and other cereals during the rainy season before moving with their herds and families. The Tigre has a rich oral literature of fairy tales, fables, riddles, poetry, and stories of war and supernatural power. They are also known for their singing and dancing. Tigre has a highly stratified society traditionally ruled by a hereditary village leader.

As in other parts of the world, Islam in Eritrea is connected with Arabic and latter evokes strong feeling among Eritrean Muslim communities. Arabic has become a part of Eritrean Muslim culture. They mainly use Arabic in their religious affairs. There are also some groups of people with clear evidence of their Arabic Origin. These are Rashaida, Addi-Mualim, Addi-sheikh, and Beit Mala.

Rashaida has migrated to the northern Eritrean and Sudanese coast in last 150 years. They live in tightly-knit, patrilineal clans. Rashaida women are noted for their red and black patterned dresses and long heavy veils often embroidered with silver, beads, and seed pearls.[13]

The area what is known as Eritrea today has been the home of variety of ethnic groups with diverse cultural traditions for millennia. It has been a passage way for human migration since time immemorial. In the process, the diverse elements and blood got mixed through historical intermarrying. Even though the country is small in size, it is among the most heterogeneous areas in the Horn of Africa linguistically, ethnically, and culturally. Broadly, the cotemporary Eritrean population could be classified into three ethnic stocks. But, it is difficult to say that today there exist a pure Nilotic or Cushitic or Semitic race in Eritrea due to thousands of years of migrations and intermingling.[14]

ENDNOTES

1. The evidence for Eritrea is found in Egyptian and Greek sources.
2. The Nilotic belongs to Nilo-Saharan language phylum.
3. It refers to south-eastern Sudan.
4. Sometimes they are referred as Barya and Baza.
5. They are recent converts from traditional African religions.
6. The northeast Africa is believed to have been the cradle of Afro-Asiatic Cushitic family of language.
7. In fact, the waves of Cushitic migration forced the Nilotics inhabitants to make internal migration.
8. Agew speakers are found deep inside the north-west Ethiopia.
9. They are mainly Roman Catholics.
10. This migration was especially from present Yemen area.
11. It hold true especially in case of the central plateau or Kebassa.
12. It is especially true among the Mensa.
13. It is obvious that their spread, settlement, and intermingling in such a vast area must have occurred over a long period of time. Unfortunately, there is lack of sufficient evidences at present which would allow us to chart their evolution in a precise manner.
14. The Rashaida ethnic group claim to be pure Semitic race. Generally, they are recent immigrant from Yemen.

5

Prehistory

The archaeological evidences that has been found in different parts of Eritrea shows that it has a long history of human settlement since the Stone Age. In fact, the present Eritrean territory seems to have played a very significant role in the historical development of the Horn of Africa as well as the dispersal of modern humans from Africa to rest of the world. As we know, there is a widely held belief that the modern humans originated in Africa. There is also a general agreement among scholars that Homo sapiens first emerged in eastern Africa around 150000 years ago and then dispersed to other parts of the world.

But, there is lack of consensus upon their route of dispersal out of Africa. Regarding this scholars are mainly divided into two main groups. The two main routes suggested are the "Northern Route" and the "Southern Route". The proponents of the former propose the Nile Basin as the principal corridor through which early humans dispersed from northeastern Africa up to the Sinai land bridge and then into Eurasia through the east Mediterranean Levant corridor. (Bar-Yosef and Belfer-Cohen 2001; Tchernov 1992).

The supporter of the "Southern Route" advocates migration from Africa to Asia through the Horn of Africa. This is also called Yemen route through the southern Red Sea area, via the Bab al Mandab. (Ambrose 2003; Kingdon 1993; Macaulay, et al. 2005; Rose 2004a). The argument in favour of this route has been strengthened by discovery of similarity in the Paleolithic assemblages from Horn of Africa, the Arabian Peninsula, and India. (Brandt 1986; Petraglia 2003; Rose 2004b; Walter, et al. 2000). This has been further corroborated by a recent genetic study which indicates rapid coastal expansion of early modern humans toward Southeast Asia around 60000 years ago. (Macaulay, et al. 2005). If the "Southern Route" migration theory holds true then one can only imagine the importance of Eritrea in prehistoric research. The strategic location of Eritrea in this "Southern Route" indicates the possible role played by this region in the dispersal of modern humans throughout the world.

Moreover, the East African Great Rift System has been the most fertile ground for the discovery of humanity's ancient cultural and physical remains. (Johanson and Edgar 1996; McDougall, et al. 2005; Semaw, et al. 1997). Eritrea encompasses part of this East African Rift System. The Rift Valley cuts northward through the mid-eastern portion of Eritrea, forming the Red Sea Basin and the Danakil depression.

THE EVOLUTION OF HUMAN SPECIES

Present human's ancestral line evolved within Africa. The *Kenyapithecus* (14000000 years ago) found in Kenya belonged to this main pre-hominid line. It was followed by Australopithecines (3800000 years ago). These were biped and so true hominids. It had various species such as *Australopithecus afarensis*[1] and *Australopithecus africanus.*[2] Latter was gracile[3] species with a cranial capacity of 500 cc. *Australopithecus africanus* is dated back to 2300000 years ago. It also comes anatomically very close to the first true human species called *Homo habilis.* Latter is found in both East and South Africa from 2600000-1700000 years ago. It was more intelligent than preceding hominid as *Homo habilis* possessed greater cranial capacity of 700 cc. It made Oldowan[4] tools. *Homo habilis* possibly lived some kind of collective life and used a series of sounds.

It had a younger cotemporary in *Homo erectus,* also called *Homo ergaster* (1800000-200000 years ago) in Africa. There is a possibility that it might be even older than 2000000 years ago. *Homo erectus* was far more robust than *Homo habilis.* It enjoyed heavy skull and greater cranial capacity, about 1000 cc. *Homo ergaster* used fire for the first time and the tools of *Homo habilis* but with greater sophistication. They shaped not only the cores but also the flakes. It gave rise to a flaked pebble tool industry. Finally, the hand axe appeared, in which the stone had two sloping sides. Therefore, it was bifacial. The technique of making such hand axes is called Acheulian. The earliest dated appearance of the hand axe is at Konso in Ethiopia, almost 1400000 years ago. Both the Oldowan and the Acheulian techniques belong to the Lower or Early Paleolithic Age.

PALEOLITHIC AGE IN ERITREA

A large number of stone tool sites belonging to middle Paleolithic have been recorded in the Qohaito plateau area.[5] (Libsekal 2008). Der'a Hawatsu[6] and the surrounding region have also been inhabited since ancient times. There are evidences of pre as well as proto-historic activities[7] in the area. (Kahsay, et al. 2008).

The Danakil region of Eritrea is home to some of the important prehistoric sites from Pleistocene[8] contexts. (Abbate, et al. 2004; Bruggemann, et al. 2004). In fact, there are wide-ranging prehistoric sites located in this region. It seems that humans occupied the Buri Peninsula and Gulf of Zula coastal areas[9] intermittently during several prehistoric periods. One of the site in this area known as Buya has produced a *Homo erectus* cranium. (Abbate, et al. 1998).

Geologically, the Buya area is very promising for discovery of new homo fossils.[10] The northern part of the Danakil[11] depression of Eritrea has resulted into discovery of numerous early Pleistocene vertebrate[12] and archaeological sites within a thick fluvio-lacustrine[13] composite succession, outcropping near the village of Buya.[14] (Abbate, et al. 1998). The sites are believed to form the most concentrated and extensive prehistoric locality for the one million years old chronology anywhere in the world. (Medin in Melake ed. 2008).

The one million years age of the Buya cranium fills a gap between the early African *Homo erectus* (2.2-1.4 million years) and the later African *Homo hiedelbergensis*[15] (0.65 million years). The brain size of the Buya homo is 750-800 cc. The two incisors[16] are highly abraded.[17] It seems that the cranium and the incisors belong to a female adult individual. The site also yields fossil remains belonging to relatives of modern elephants, hippopotamus, rhinoceros, waterbuck, giraffe, and crocodiles etc. The large mammal assemblage represents a late early Pleistocene association of the East African Rift. The type of mammalian is predominantly composed of taxa[18] with strong water dependence and typical of more open landscapes.

The Buya area has also yielded lithic assemblages mainly consisting of hand-axes, choppers, and flakes. The majority of the lithic are referred to the Acheulian[19] technology and attributed to homo bearing level. According to researchers, the late Early Pleistocene human remains from Uadi Alad present the very earliest evidence of human presence in the region and likely to constitute one of the most striking paleo-anthropological discoveries in the entire African record.

The Abdur Reef Complex along the Gulf of Zula coast too has yielded Paleolithic artifacts. Latter consists of Acheulian hand axes,[20] chert, and obsidian flakes and blades.[21] It provides the oldest indications of coastal adaptations by middle-upper Pleistocene humans. It seems that the human foraging activities varied with environmental setting in this area. (Bruggemann, et al. 2004). The different cultural phases indicate the varied human adaptive strategies to climatic fluctuation in the later Pleistocene and early Holocene. (Beyin and Shea in Schmidt, et al. ed. 2008).

The tools like prismatic[22] blades, bidirectional and unidirectional blade cores; Levallois[23] flakes and cores, microliths, and non-diagnostic shatter has been found in Buri Peninsula.[24] Technologically, blade production dominates in most of the sites.

Middle Paleolithic Age[25] artifacts dominate three main sites such as Asfet, Kusrale 3, and Asadaf East. According to the researches till recently, Upper Paleolithic Ag[26] sites seem to be better represented in the area. Sites with blade production constitute the majority. Moreover, obsidian seems to be the dominant raw material at the majority of the discovered sites.

The Buri Peninsula and Gulf of Zula coastal areas provide an important view of human coastal adaptation around the Red Sea coast from the middle to early Pleistocene. It further confirms the presence of rich Paleolithic archaeological traces in the area and its intermittent occupation. They also substantiate the model of coastal adaptation[27] of early humans especially the Pleistocene-age coastal adaptations in northeast Africa. The Red Sea coast would have been a favourable location for human settlement during glacial periods, when adjacent interior regions at higher elevations were desertified, if the coastal oasis model is right. (Beyin and Shea in Schmidt, et al. ed. 2008).

MESOLITHIC AND NEOLITHIC AGE IN ERITREA

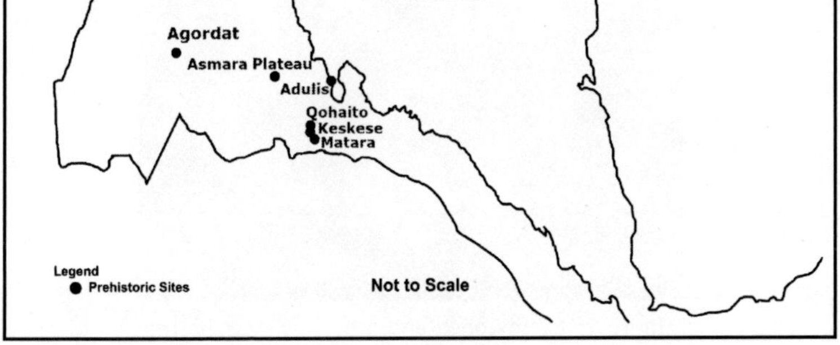

Map 1: The important prehistoric sites in Eritrea and northern Ethiopia

The microlithic[28] industries have been recorded not only in Eritrea but also in Tigray, Begemeder (Gonder), and Gojam areas of present day Ethiopia. The evidence from Gobedra (Tigray) has been dated to the 7th millennium BCE.

A test excavation[29] was conducted at Kokan site near Agordat area in the early nineties of the last century (Figure 2). This site is similar to the Late Neolithic industry of east-central Sudan. Kokan lithic shares a number of characteristics with Gash Group sites of eastern Sudan. Its typical tool assemblage includes end and side scrapers, notches,[30] denticulate,[31] backed tools, and crescents.[32] (Fattovich 1993). Kokan and the other Agordat sites are dated to at least the Egyptian New Kingdom. They are tied socially, politically, and economically to pastoral and agro-pastoral, and urban communities of Nubia and perhaps even Egypt.

Figure 2: Grindstones and other artifacts on the deflated surface near Kokan hill

Agordat sites have been included into a model of Gash Group[33] subsistence, settlement, and socioeconomic patterns. (Fattovich 1993). Kokan habitation firmly places the Agordat sites within the mix of all these regional trading systems from their beginnings in the middle Gash phase around 2300 BCE[34] to the Pre-Aksumite period, c. 400 BCE.[35] (Sadr 1991).

The ceramics from this site indicate that the western Eritrea was influenced by a number of nomadic pastoral or agro-pastoral cultures from eastern Sudan directly or indirectly since late Holocene period. It also shows the presence of some local archaeological culture(s). These Agordat communities[36] were engaged in herding and some cultivation. In the 4th-3rd millennium BCE, the Eritrean-Sudanese borderland has been an area for cattle breeding. This practice of cattle breeding was believed to start around 4000 BCE. As research in the Gash Delta have demonstrated that by the 2nd millennium BCE, the western Eritrean lowland and namely the middle Barka valley were already inhabited by nomadic and semi nomadic indigenous population. The most astonishing records of animal husbandry in pre-historical Eritrea are presented by the rock paintings discovered in Karora area and in Akkele Guzai.[37] In these places depictions of short horned and humpless cattle and anthropomorphic figures are found.

Some researchers have suggested that food production might have started in the 7th millennium BCE. It seems that the present Eritrean region was an independent center of plant domestication. The earliest evidence for plant domestication has been found at Gobedra (Tigray). It consisted of a few finger millet seeds and a tooth of Camel, tentatively dated to around 4000 BCE (ELF). In addition to this, wheat and barley were introduced by the inhabitants of the area around Agordat. And with the cultivation of the earliest cereals; ploughshare, pottery and grinding stones began to appear.

The Agordat communities would have played a very important role in the region due to the social, economic, and political conduits between the polities of eastern Sudan and the Nile Valley. The increasingly more complex socio-political systems emerged in the Eritrean highlands such as the Pre-Aksumite and Ancient Ona. (Steven A. Brandt, Andrea Manzo, and Cinzia Perlingieri in Peter R. Schmidt, Matthew C. Curtis, and Zelalem Teka ed. 2008).

Some scholars and researchers have recently proposed the Horn of Africa as a launching point for circum-Indian Ocean dispersal. (Kingdon 1993; Stringer 2002). Eritrea lies along the major biogeographic route of migration into and out of Africa. It is possible that Eritrea's prehistoric heritage includes some of the last common ancestors of Africans and non-Africans. (Beyin and Shea in Peter R. Schmidt, Matthew C. Curtis, and Zelalem Teka ed. 2008). Field researches in Sudan and Ethiopia has revealed fossils of the oldest Homo sapiens and evidence for the early appearance of modern human behaviour. (McDougall, et al. 2005; McBrearty and Brooks 2000).

It is plausible that the future archaeological and paleo-anthropological researches in Eritrea will add to these discoveries and contribute data on early coastal adaptations. It may also shed further light on the origin and dispersal of modern humans. (Beyin and Shea in Peter R. Schmidt, Matthew C. Curtis, and Zelalem Teka ed. 2008). Buya site is probably one of the most interesting findings in the African continent. But, there are still extensive unexplored areas with the potential to put Eritrea paleontologically in its rightful place. The above mentioned Prehistoric remains clearly demonstrates that the earliest inhabitants of this region were enjoying a complex socio-economic and cultural systems. The end of Prehistory in this region can be put at about the coming of the south Arabian immigrants and the introduction of inscription.

ENDNOTES

1. It is found in east Africa. Lucy is one of its examples found in Ethiopia.
2. It is found in South Africa.

3. It means gracefully slim and slight.
4. It is made by striking one stone against another and so breaking flakes off pebbles to obtain cutting edges in the cores.
5. Moreover, some scholars believe that Qohaito plateau might have been in use since a long time if not inhabited by human communities. Such kind of activity may date back to as early as the Pleistocene and early Holocene.
6. Broadly, the Der'a Hawatsu area could be divided into two parts. One part is located in the Arato plateau and its escarpment. The other one is located on the rugged topography alongside the mountain chains of river Hadas. The area is located adjacent to the ancient city of Qohaito and nearby to the northern trade route of the Hadas and Kumalie rivers. Perhaps, this was a conjunction area of trade route that connected the central highlands with the ancient cities of the southern hinterlands and the Red Sea coast. The topography is mainly dominated by mountains, hills, and deep valleys. There is high fluctuation in elevation. The area is endowed with several seasonal and perennial streams. The region is predominantly covered with acacia, grass, juniper trees, and other bushes. The main rock types are schist and sandstone.
7. Der'a Hawatsu region is endowed with very rich and diverse archaeological materials. Most of the archaeological sites in the area are situated on top of the hills and mountains and located near the seasonal or perennial streams. Probably, the mainstay of their economy was agriculture and pastoralism. The major archaeological findings include ruined settlement walls, fallen columns, terraces, kilns, an underground walled tunnel, potsherds, inscriptions, and rock arts. As far as the ceramic type is concerned, the potsherds are red slipped in the outside and simple or plain red inside. A monumental architecture has also been found on top of the mountain north of the Ahune village. The lithic industry includes flakes, scrapers, and cores of quartz and obsidian. One also finds the evidence of numerous grinding stones indicating cereal processing. The rock inscription is inscribed with Sabaean script. The Der'a Hawatsu area is rich in archaeological materials with lot of diversity. One of the most interesting findings is the plastered wall and the terrace. Latter might imply the management of soil in the ancient times.

8. Pleistocene is the epoch of geologic time, about 1.6 million to 10,000 years ago. It is characterized by the disappearance of continental ice sheets and the appearance of humans.
9. It is located in the northern part of the Danakil depression.
10. This is due to its depositional and tectonic setting similar to the Middle Awash region of Ethiopia.
11. It is inhabited by Afar people.
12. Vertebrates are animal with backbone. It is an animal with a segmented spinal column and a well developed brain such as mammal, bird, reptile, amphibian, or fish etc.
13. It is related to rivers and lakes.
14. It is about 100 kilometer south of Massawa port city.
15. *Homo heidelbergensis* is one form of early humans. It travelled into Europe some time before 800,000 years ago. Their migration represents an ability and desire of early humans to roam outside Africa and settle on other continents.
16. Incisors are flat sharp front tooth. It is one of the flat sharp-edged teeth in front of the mouth generally used for cutting and tearing food.
17. It refers to wearing away.
18. It refers to a category of organisms. Precisely speaking, it indicates a group to which organisms are assigned according to the principles of taxonomy, including species, genus, family, order, class, and phylum.
19. By 1.5 million years ago, early humans had begun to make new kinds of tools, which archaeologists call *Acheulian.* These tools were finely crafted, larger, and more symmetrical. The common Acheulian tools included large hand axes and cleavers. These tools might have helped early humans in hunting.
20. These hand axes are found in association with oyster beds.
21. These chert and obsidian flakes and blades have been found in connection with fossils of large terrestrial mammals. It has been attributed to Middle Paleolithic Age.
22. It means something brightly coloured resembling a prism.
23. Levallois is a type of artifacts which has been named after a suburb of Paris, where for the first time it was discovered. This is a method through which flakes of a predetermined shape were removed from specially

prepared cores. This process resulted in oval-shaped flakes or large triangular points depending on the type of Levallois core. Levallois cores and flakes are first seen at some late Acheulian sites but become much more common in the Middle Paleolithic.

24. It refers to artifacts which break suddenly into many small brittle pieces.
25. It is also referred to as Middle Stone Age in African context.
26. It is also referred to as Later Stone Age in African context.
27. According to this model, during glacial events, when sea level dropped several meters below the present level, the discharge of fresh water from terrestrial aquifers created favourable habitats along the Red Sea coast. During the glacial episodes, when nearby inland habitats deteriorated, fresh water springs are created along the exposed coastal landscapes, thus creating new habitats for terrestrial mammals and humans. (Faure, et al. 2002).
28. The Microlithic tool industry refers to Mesolithic Age. Generally speaking, Mesolithic Age extends from the end of the Pleistocene Ice Age, about 10,000 years ago, until the Neolithic Age (period when farming became central to a peoples' livelihood), which occurred at different times around the world. The term Mesolithic is generally applied to the period of post-Pleistocene hunting and gathering. Mesolithic sites are usually characterized by microliths. Microlithic blade segments were commonly retouched into a range of shapes, including crescents, triangles, rectangles, and trapezoids and thus the tools are often called geometric microliths. These forms often have multiple sharp edges. Many of these microliths probably served as elements of composite tools, such as blade-tipped spears or arrows, or wooden-handled knives. The microliths were likely inserted into shafts or handles of wood or antler and reinforced with some type of adhesive.
29. Berhane Tesfamariam and Danny Defla (staff members of National Museum of Eritrea) and Steven Brandt conducted a test excavation at this site in 1994.
30. It refers to a tool with a small V-shaped cut or indentation in an edge or surface.
31. It means a tool with fine teeth or pointed projections.
32. These crescents are made from bipolar and other cores of quartz and more rarely chert and basalt etc.

33. Beginning around 2500 BCE, pastoralists or agro-pastoralists from the Butana region (east of the Nile) began to move east. They eventually established large permanent villages along the Gash River and its channels. They were dependent on cattle, goats, and sheep, and perhaps cereals as well as wild game and plant foods. They also migrated north into the Red Sea hills. By 2000 BCE, these chiefdom-level societies were engaged in contact and probable trade with Kerma and C-Group peoples in the Middle Nile Valley. The Gash Group people continued to move east and occupied the entire Sudan-Eritrean borderland, including Agordat. Farming and herding were the main subsistence activities. Gash Group people were included in the large circuit of economic interchanges gradually evolving between the peoples of Egypt, Sudan, Ethiopia, and perhaps Somalia and southern Arabia. However, by late 800 BCE, trading systems shifted away from the Nile towards the Eritrean Highlands and the Red Sea.
34. At this time they may have been located on the eastern periphery of the Gash core.
35. By this time Agordat would have been more centrally positioned to reap the benefits of increasing trade between the Nile Valley and Eritrean highlands.
36. They were probably Nilo-Saharan speaking agro-pastoralists.
37. These rock paintings are found in the sites between Mai Aini and Sen'afe. It includes Sellum Ba'atti, Zeban Ona, and Emba Foqada.

6

Rock Art

Eritrea is endowed with a vast heritage of rock art sites. It is believed that this ancient land has the most concentration of rock art sites in the Horn of Africa. (Negash 1997). These rock art sites are spread throughout the country. But, its size and distribution vary widely. Some of them are found in northern part of the country (Qarora), others on the western lowlands (Agordat area) and a few on the southeastern lowlands (Rahaita). However, the most and widely known concentration is located in the highland plateau of the southern region. (Map 2).

Map 2: The distribution of ancient rock art sites in Eritrea

PHYSICAL DISTRIBUTION

The western lowlands in general and the area around the town of Haicota and the Barka River valley in particular possess some invaluable ancient rock art. Three localities such as Cullite, Dinae, and Elit in this area have produced rock paintings and engravings of humans and animals as well as abstract designs. (Calegari 1999). The northern part of the country, especially the sites such as Ciakat, Nagran, and Deudeu around Karora and Rora area have produced rock art consisting of a number of panels with depictions of cattle, goats, and sheep as well as geometric designs. (Calegari 1999). Some of the sites in central part of the country such as Baati Mariam, Daaro Paulos, Wuanttebba, Mehba Worki, Harom, Lortamit, Maji Malehesss, Lamdrara, and Dembe Wadi Mudui have produced rock engravings consisting of human figures, animals, and some abstract designs. (Cervicek 1976). Eastern lowlands have produced some of the rock art such as rock engraving consisting of schematic depictions of camels and other geometric designs. (Calegari 1999).

The southern region of the country as mentioned earlier, especially the town of Adikeih and its surroundings is endowed with the largest concentration of rock art in this country (Figure 3-3.2).

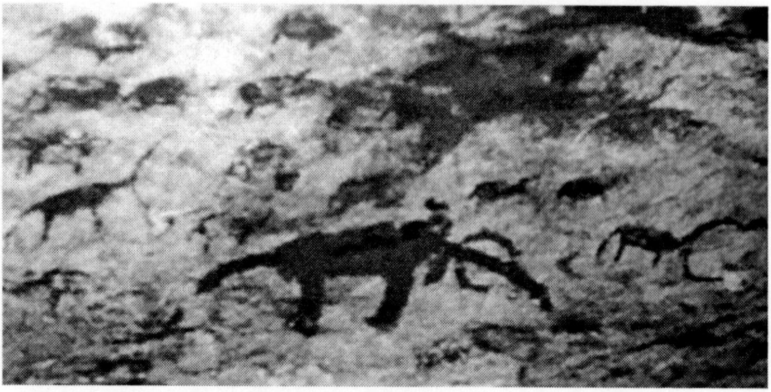

Figure 3: Rock painting of elephant like animal and other mammals in the Hishmele rock shelter north of Adikeih.

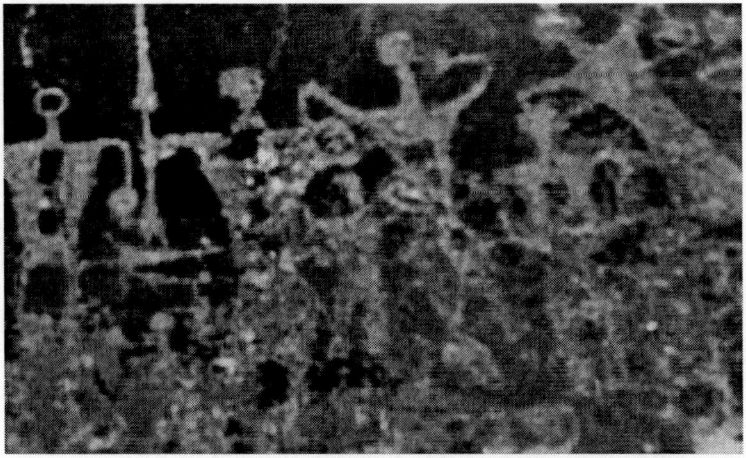

Figure 3.1: An example of realistic engravings from Me'alewaya near the town of Adikeih depicting simple human figures with open raised arms and with a tool.

Figure 3.2: The geometric and abstract paintings (lines, dot, group of dots, and circle etc) from Helum Bareto, north of the town of Adikeih.

Qohaito is another area in this region which is endowed with some of the most famous rock art sites such as Adi Alewti, Iyago, Karibosa, and Hadamu (Figure 3.4-3.6).

Figure 3.3: The depiction of elephants on a cliff-face to the east of the Qohaito plateau.

The rock art in Adi Alewti can be classified into two groups. There are rock paintings of two colours such as white[1] and red. The rock engravings mainly consist of inscriptions and monographs. The paintings are simple naturalistic representations of animals and very rarely humans. The most depicted animals are domestic long horned cattle and camels. One finds broad uniformity and homogeneity[2] in the engravings. (Zemuy in Melake ed. 2008).

Figure 3.4: The portrayal of a herd of cattle and camels in Addi Alewti on the Qohaito Plateau.

Iyago consists of dozens of painted forms on the walls of the rock shelter. The nature of the rock[3] indicates a deliberate geological choice by the artists. The representations are painted in only hematite

Figure 3.5: Paintings at Iyago in the Qohaito Plateau.

reddish brown coloured pigment. They portray mainly cattle such as long horned and unidentified animals. These animals are generally mounted by other depictions including humans with longer genital organs, with lowered, raised and open arms and in some instances with sticks. Generally speaking, the rock painting in Qohaito comprises representations of livestock and depictions of humans. Some rock engravings consist of inscriptions of Ge'ez and Sabean, where as, some rare monographs and abstract paintings. (Zemuy in Melake ed. 2008).

The Der'a Hawatsu area[4] is very rich in rock art. More than a dozen rock art sites have been found in the region. They are located in caves of bedrock slopes. The sites are mainly found on sandstone rocks. The rock paintings include the images of animals, humans, alphabet-like and other indistinguishable figures. Animal images are dominated by cattle. They are depicted with long and twisted horns. Their horns, legs, and tails are well represented. This might indicate the domestication of wild cattle or buffalo like animals. Generally, the artists have tried to maintain the proportionality in their piece of art. The cattle are shown in folk either one after the other or side-by-side. This may denote the possession of more than one cattle by some individuals. Wherever they are painted as a single animal, it is very big and could have some ritual meaning.

The human representations are generally found with cattle. This may represent the herders. Artists have taken great care in showing position and instrument as well. In one of the paintings, two individuals holding a shield in their hands have been depicted. This may point towards the existence of raid and defensive mechanism during the period. One also observes the wheeled cart consisting of wheel and chair. The isolated alphabets resembling to Sabaean script are scattered over the cave walls. One of the interesting paintings is the two circular lines of concentric circles in red and dark blue colours radiating from the centre. The artists have mainly used red colour except in one case where dark blue colour exists. There could be several reasons for that. One might be that the red color was easily accessible to them. Other could be the resistance power of this colour towards change. Another plausible reason could be that the red was the colour of painted cattle. Its rich rock art might throw important lights on several issues such as the origin of animal domestication and cave painting or its diffusion in the area, and the relationship between human beings and animals. (Kahsay, et al. in Melake ed. 2008).

SETTING, STYLE, CONTENT, MEANING AND SIGNIFICANCE

Some researcher has divided these rock arts into three broad groups such as realistic, geometric paintings and engravings, and abstract paintings and engravings. The physical context of realistic paintings is vertical cliffs lining major valleys that offer panoramic view of the valley below (Figure 3.3). Some of these sites are difficult to reach, whereas others are located along major human occupation sites. The art located in open and easily accessible settings is usually associated with permanent water sources, and is frequently well above the canyon floors. As far as the content of the realistic paintings are concerned, it consists of carefully reproduced scenes of both everyday and special activities (Figures 3, 3.1, 3.3, 3.4, and 3.5).

Depictions include animals and humans both as isolated elements and as parts of larger scenes. It contains communal pastoralism, rituals, and group of animals. The figures are uniform in style as well as scale. They are detailed and finely executed. There are also superimpositions that are probably intended to renew a fading panel. Some art probably depict hunting related rituals such as dancing humans with elaborate headdresses or masks and usually with erect phalluses. Historians have offered several justifications for these realistic rock art. They may have been casual drawings to pass the time while waiting for game or decoration of living spaces, hallucination, recording of events important to the group or an educational device.[5] (Teka in Peter R. Schmidt, Matthew C. Curtis, and Zelalem Teka ed. 2008).

The geometric paintings and engravings occur in both easily accessible canyons as well as in areas that are difficult to reach (Figure 3.3). It is usually found on exposed outcrops alongside and sometimes within panels of other styles. Generally, it seems non-representational with few exceptions. In fact, no patterning is observed in the arrangement or repetition of individual elements. Most of the abstract paintings and engravings occur in less-accessible and hard-to-reach localities. But sometimes, it is also found in readily accessible spots along major river canyons.

It seems that no particular surface was favoured in this case. It also shows little physical and spatial patterning. This rock style shows simple, repetitious, and generally symmetrical designs. It seems that no attention was given to the natural boundaries of rock surfaces. It may represent phosphene art.[6] (Pearson 2002). This specific style can also be accredited to ritual or shamanistic[7] activity. (Lewis-Williams 1986, 1991; Pearson 2002). Such altered state of perception is typical of ritual or liminal states. Therefore, it seems reasonable to draw a connection between rock art depicting phosphenes and shamanism or some forms of nonspecific ritual activity.

Thus one can say that Eritrea is one of the richest countries in terms of rock art heritage. In its rock art, the animal figures dominate with some depictions of humans as well. Moreover, the rock art of

Eritrea belongs to the broad Ethiopian-Arabian style of the Horn.[8] Its art is associated with cattle herding or pastoralism. It may fit to the cultural ecological model of cattle herding suggested by Steven A. Brandt and Nancy Carder.

ENDNOTES

1. It is the dominant colour out of the two.
2. It may be due to execution by pecking with finely pointed chisel or iron or stone that was stroked by another instrument.
3. The artist seems to have preferred sandstone over other rocks.
4. The Der'a Hawatsu area is located on the south-eastern highland in the southern region of Eritrea.
5. A trainee could be made familiar with certain beliefs and practices of the group through this.
6. It is an art produced under conditions of sensory deprivation or enhancement.
7. It refers to an animistic belief system involving shamans. Latter are spiritual leaders believed to have special power of prophecy or healing. Shamanism was especially in vogue in northern Asia, in which shamans are believed to be able to intercede between humanity and powerful good and evil spirits.
8. Cerevick described it as showing the body and legs of the cattle in profile. The fore legs and hind legs are each pooled to one thick line. The hoofs are sometimes stylized to resemble pincers but more often, the legs have rounded ends dismissing the hooves entirely. The head, neck, and the horn of the animals are shown from the back like with a bovid which turns its head from on-looker.

7

Pre and Proto-Aksumite Era

Broadly speaking, the "Pre-Aksumite" culture flourished between 900 BCE-300 BCE. During this period, the Eritrean plateau and Tigray entered into early historical period preceding the rise of Aksum and thus called the "Pre-Aksumite" period. Its cultural area stretches from the Rora plateau in northern Eritrea to Enderta in Tigray. Anfray distinguished two main developmental stages in the "Pre-Aksumite" period such as the South Arabian[1] period (c.500 BCE-300 BCE) and the Intermediary period (c. 300 BCE-100 BCE). Latter is also designated as "Proto-Aksumite" cultural period by some scholars.

PRE-AKSUMITE CULTURE

"Pre-Aksumite Period" saw the growth of complex urban-like settlement system in northern Tigray, central highlands, Asmara Plateau, and Akkele Guzai region of Eritrea. These settlements included domestic as well as specialized administrative[2] and religious centers.[3] Not surprisingly, most of these urban settlements were located in relatively fertile and well-watered area. The "Pre-Aksumite" period is characterized by specialized craft production, sophisticated ceramic traditions; elaborate monumental and domestic architectural forms, and writing system etc. (Anfray 1968, 1990; Curtis 2004; de Contenson 1981; Fattovich 1990, 2000; Phillipson 1998, 2000; Schmidt and Curtis 2001).

The "Pre-Aksumite Period" communities practiced agro-pastoral subsistence economies. They cultivated cereal crops and legumes such as barely, wheat, linseed, lentils, and tef; and raised domesticated cattle, goats, and sheep. (Boardman 1999, 2000; Cain 2000; Curtis 2004, 2005; D'Andrea, et al. 1999, 2002; Schmidt 2002a; Schmidt and Curtis 2001).

From 1000 BCE to 400 BCE, Eritrea and Tigray plateau experienced concentrated migration of population from south Arabia. But this immigration and settlement processes took long time. The main Semitic influx took place, when the south Arabia was at the climax of its civilization. The cultural influences of those immigrants can be deduced from several archaeological sites in Eritrea and Tigray. They introduced *Mukarrib* system along with the monopoly of power in the hands of the king.[4] These immigrants contributed to artificial irrigation system, dams, hydraulic devices, and terrace farming in agricultural field. As far as architecture is concerned, they seemed to have introduced towers; multi storey palaces; and rectangular stone walled and roofed houses. The acculturation processes between the new immigrants and the pre-existing Cushitic elements seemed to have contributed to the evolution of Geez.[5] The Sabaean brought more sophisticated religion especially the complex polytheistic aspect. The new settlers built several temples of their most important Gods.[6]

Matara belongs to both "Pre-Aksumite" as well as Aksumite period. The "Pre-Aksumite" level[7] of the site is reported to have produced small bowls with an exterior molded lip, small cups with carinated profiles, and small jars with everted[8] rim and cross-hatching rhomboidal[9] designs along the shoulder. The common ceramic vessel types from Matara include cream ware amphorae; black burnished cups,[10] and large jar forms.[11] (Anfray 1966, 1967; Anfray and Annequin 1965; Fattovich 1980, 1990). According to Fattovich, these ceramics types are comparable to those found at the Ancient Ona site[12] of Ona Hashel. (Anfray 1970). The other "Pre-Aksumite" related evidences are the inscriptions referring to several Gods and Goddesses like Dat-Badan,[13] Athtar, Almaqah,[14] and star deity etc; libation altar with the south Arabian script *mtryn*; and several assumed sacrificial altars.[15]

Qohaito has the possibilities of "Pre-Aksumite" as well as early-Aksumite settlements. (Wolf 1997). The ceramic evidence includes "Pre-Aksumite" potsherds. These ceramics[16] consists of black-topped red ware. Like Matara and Qohaito, Keskese also represents "Pre-Aksumite" settlements. It consists of at least 10 archaeological sites.[17] The site has been described as a "Pre-Aksumite" ceremonial center due to six rectangular monolithic pillars[18] or obelisks. A tomb burial, three coils of bronze, and a large schist monolith have also been reported from the site.[19] As far as its lithic industry is concerned, the chipped stone artifact tools including scrapers, perforators, retouched flake tools; and crescents and geometric microliths have been discovered from its surface.

Most of its ceramics are red wares.[20] Interestingly like Matara, there exists some similarity between the ceramic assemblages at Keskese and Ancient Ona sites in Greater Asmara area. The remnants of substantial monumental architecture, multiple large mound features, a notable inscription, and abundant "Pre-Aksumite" ceramic and lithic materials suggest a dynamic setting, where both settlement and ritual and ceremonial activities took place over many years. However, such feature along with the evidence of past agricultural terraces, wells, and pathways across the site suggest complex patterns of site use.

Another "Pre-Aksumite" site Addi Gramaten is located just west of Keskese near the head of the Haddas Valley in the Akkele Guzai region. The site has produced a stone sphinx statue, small stone slab, and stepped base altar with an Epigraphic south Arabian inscription. The stone sphinx statue measured 13 inches in length, 6.5 inches in width, and 9.5 inches in height. It depicts a male lion's body with a human head and a double necklace of amulet-like objects and a one word south Arabian inscription on the right leg. Its hair is shaped in plaits.

Interestingly, the stepped slab altar was found close to the sphinx. It included a recessed decoration on its top and three brief

South Arabian inscriptions located along the altar frieze. A "Pre-Aksumite" piriform-shaped red ware vessels similar to Ancient Ona ware,[21] some unidentified red ware ceramic sherds, a brick-like object, a mud mortar stone wall, stone architectural rubble, and slate have either been recovered or exposed at the Addi Gramaten site. According to Fattovich, this site might have served as a cultural border mark.

Figure 4: A sphinx like statue from Addi Gramaten, recovered in 1945.

Fiqya[22] is located southwest of present town of Senafe and almost 10 km from Matara. The site has been dated to "Pre-Aksumite" cultural period. (Anfray 1965). It consists of building structures with walls constructed largely form schist rock and rectangular shaped offering table with two projecting broken stone sphinx-like figures, "Pre-Aksumite" temple structure, and inscriptions engraved in stone blocks. (Drewes 1954, 1956, 1962). However, the combination of the architecture, offering table, and inscriptions suggests that the site may represent a "Pre-Aksumite" ceremonial centre. (Fattovich 1990).

PROTO-AKSUMITE CULTURE

In fact, one finds the beginning of change in the central elements of complex society in northern Horn by 4th century BCE. These changes are seen in material culture and spatial characteristics of domestic settlements and ceremonial sites. Therefore, there was cultural transformation that preceded the rise of the Aksumite culture and state formation in the region. But nevertheless, there were certain continuities as well as changes in socio-economic and cultural milieu[23] between the "Pre-Aksumite" and "Proto-Aksumite Period."

During this period, the south Arabians of the earlier stage have been assimilated to local conditions, and synthesization process between the indigenous and new immigrant provided for the development of the distinctly Eritrean and Tigrean style. Broadly speaking, it is the period of acculturation which led the foundation stone to the Aksumite civilization.

FOREIGN RELATION

This was also the period when Eritrea and Tigray region enjoyed important relationship with several contemporary civilized societies of the world namely Egypt, Greek, Meroe, and Israel etc. The Egyptian sources referred this territory as the "Land of Kush" or the "Land of Punt."[24] The Egyptian ruler's contact with this region goes back to very ancient times. The Pharaohs launched numerous commercial and exploitative expeditionary missions towards this area. On their way; some of the explorers, traders, and adventurers wrote interesting account of the history and culture of the area, and the impact it experienced due to its contacts with outside world.[25] From the 4th century BCE onwards, with the rise and expansion of Hellenistic culture and political hegemony, the task of expeditions passed on to the new rulers in Egypt, the Ptolemies.

The Greek established an empire between the 4th and 2nd century BCE. They invaded Egypt and made it as their overseas colony for more than two centuries. The Greek rulers in Egypt were known as Ptolemy. As their predecessors, the Ptolemaic merchants, sailors, and explorers made voyages to this region and wrote much useful information. For the first time, the name Eritrea appears in Greek sources referring to the Red sea.[26] The interest of the Ptolemy rulers[27] was in expanding Commercial network. To this fact, they laboured in constructing ports and trading stations.[28] Finally, they created a strong commercial, political, and cultural linkage with port of Adulis and Aksum.

In the 2nd and 1st century BCE, the Romans succeeded the Greeks in domination of the same areas. But their dream of engulfing the "Pre-Aksumite" area failed. Nevertheless, the trade contact between Romans along the Red Sea and Indian ocean routes gave a new impulse to the cultural and political development of the region. Meroe[29] had close political relation with Eritrea and Tigray. However as Aksum grew stronger, Meroe got weaker and finally gave way to the Nubia.

Israel had political and religious influence on this region in ancient times. The relation was legendary mainly based on the Old Testament of the holy Bible. It is believed that Queen of Sheba visited the king Solomon and discussed with him all that was in her heart. Solomon answered all her questions. This legend stated that the queen got pregnant from Solomon and bore her first son who was named Menilik I. He went back to Jerusalem and was educated in Israel. Although his father asked him to remain in Israel, Menilik I refused and returned back to his motherland. Solomon sent the tribes of Israel to help him rule his kingdom. In this way, the culture, religion, and political system of Israel were introduced to this region.

So, the Pre-Aksumite culture of this region developed from complex processes involving the mixture of different foreign cultures with the existing Nilotic, Cushitic, and Semitic elements. As aforementioned, the Eritrean and Tigrean civilization which took shape in the Aksumite period was mainly the result of the interaction between the local Cushitic and south Arabian Semitic elements.

ENDNOTES

1. It is also referred to as Sabean culture.
2. One of the examples of this type of site is Matara.
3. This includes ceremonial centers like Keskese, Hawelti-Melazo, and Yeha.
4. It was probably justified by the belief of the king's divine origin.
5. But this argument is refuted by several recent scholars. However, the Semitic language is spoken in slightly varying forms in present Eritrea.
6. Their main Gods were Ashter (the Sun God), Almouqah (the moon God), and Shams etc.
7. At least, two excavated strata are believed to belong to "Pre-Aksumite" period.
8. It means turning a body part outward.
9. It indicates a parallelogram shape with unequal sides.
10. These cups contain incised triangle decorative motifs along the rim and sometimes filled with white-paste.
11. These consist of vertical handles, rim grooves, and parallel molded rib elements.
12. In fact, the "Pre-Aksumite" level ceramics from Matara bear strong resemblances to characteristic ceramic from Ancient Ona sites such as piriform shaped jars, small jars with restricted necks and everted rims, and small jugs with vertical handles.
13. It may have been associated with solar cult as in south Arabia.
14. Almaqah was the moon God. This along with Athtar was an important deity and commonly represented in the southern Red Sea world of the 1st millennium BCE.
15. There are several flat stone tables that may represent sacrificial altar. (Anfray and Annequin 1965).
16. Generally, black burnished, red burnished and slipped wares are characteristic of "Pre-Aksumite Period" in the northern Horn of Africa.
17. These includes two site areas with six obelisks, another two with extensive in situ architectural wall and terrace features and substantial architectural rubble, and six smaller mound site areas. This was reported by Daniel Habtemichael who did a field research in the Keskese valley during 2001. (Habtemichael 2002, 2004).

18. They are 7-9 meters in length.
19. Giuseppe Tringali excavated the site in 1964.
20. Some of them are with red slip or red slip and black burnish. (Habtemichael 2002, 2004).
21. These Ancient Ona ware are piriform-shaped red ware vessels.
22. Alternatively, it is also known as Feqya.
23. It includes material culture, economy, and written languages.
24. It means God's land.
25. The most outstanding documentation in this connection is represented in Egyptian temple at Deir-el-Bahari. It was commissioned by Queen Hatshepsut (18th dynasty, 1520-1484 BCE).
26. Like wise, it was Greek geographers who named Ethiopia to indicate any area of the 'black world' below Egypt.
27. It included Ptolemy I Soter, Ptolemy II Philadelphus, and Ptolemy III Euergetes.
28. These were done in order to open the way to their traders, sailors, and explorers.
29. It was the capital city of ancient Kush kingdom roughly located south of the confluence of Atbara and Nile River. In the 8th century BCE, the capital of the kingdom shifted to Napata. It was one of the centers of ancient civilizations.

8

Ona Culture

Some ancient communities flourished in the highlands around Asmara between 800-400 BCE. They are popularly known as "Ancient Ona communities." The term Ona is a Tigrinya word meaning "ruins." They represent an extraordinary period in the history of Eritrea as well as Horn of Africa. These communities preceded as well as were contemporaneous to some of the Pre-Aksumite culture.[1] Moreover, these people were precursor to the mid-first millennium BCE urban development in the central highlands of Eritrea. Some of the important sites belonging to Ancient Ona communities in Greater Asmara area are Sembel, Sembel Kushet, Mai Chiot, Mai Hutsa, Ona Gudo, Weki Duba, Kehawta, and Adi Abeito etc (Figure 5).

Here, the various facets of these ancient Ona communities would be discussed. The broad characteristics of these communities including their settlement pattern, subsistence pattern, land use, tool technology, flora, fauna, and growth towards urbanism, society, and culture would be explored and analyzed.

ONA COMMUNITY

The ancient Ona community seems to have grown naturally. Asmara's advantageous position in the highland with easy accessibility to fertile water and soil; and its location at the juncture of regional trade routes created a suitable environment for the rise of these complex communities. The Greater Asmara area[2] comprised of several community clusters. Some of them consisted of central towns

Figure 5: An overview of the Sembel Ona site.

surrounded by contiguous communities involving villages, hamlets, and household units. Sometimes, these central towns were twice the size of their adjoining communities. We find both the closer as well as wider spacing[3] in the distribution of the communities in these clusters. This may be attributed to the differences in economic and other activities in those areas. (Curtis and Schmidt 2008). The ancient Ona people lived in villages and small towns made of solid stone walls. These ancient Ona communities mostly build their houses on sterile rock outcrops.[4]

Latter was also the scene of various other non-cultivation activities. The houses were attached to one another. (Schmidt, et al. 2008). They build some security outposts guarding the major roads to the lowlands. These people also made sufficient provisions of common areas for cultivation and pasturing. There were several multi-purpose sites that were used for various activities ranging from cattle corrals, agricultural rest areas, ore-processing areas, tool production and repair areas, ritual areas, and pastoral watch stations. Sometimes, these multi-purpose sites were centrally located. There were also some sites used for specific purposes such as stone quarrying, tool production, ash dumps, stone circles, and mining. The post-cultivation activities seem to have occurred near the fields. Probably, threshing took place on specially packed clay floors located in non-cultivable area.[5] These Ona people must have spent weeks on these sites with numerous associated activities.[6] Sometimes, sites seem to have been completely abandoned and the inhabitants settled in other areas. The possible reasons could be rivalries, cycles of disease, and drought etc. (Curtis and Schmidt 2008). (Figures 5.1-5.6)

Figure 5.1: A small pot decorated with incision from Weki Duba Ona site.

Figure 5.2: A brown ware pot with a handle from Ona Gudo site.

Figure 5.3: The disk and barrel shaped beads from the Mai Hutsa Ona site.

Figure 5.4: A bronze seal from Mai Chiot Ona site.

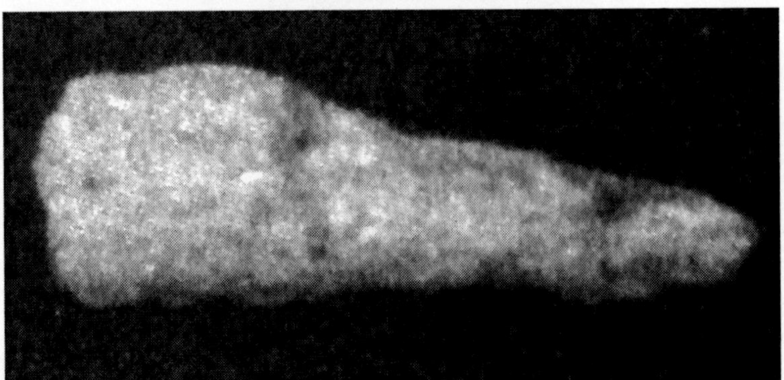

Figure 5.5: A bronze pin from Mai Chiot Ona site.

Figure 5.6: Author showing a stone artifact from Sembel Ona site.

The ancient Ona communities were sedentary people practicing a mix of subsistence economy of agriculture and pastoralism.[7] Their life centered on agricultural production and domestic stock. Initially, these people cultivated emmer, barely, durum,[8] lentils, and linseed. Later on, they went on to add tef.[9] However, the most important crops cultivated by them were emmer, barely, and linseed. Tef and lentil seems to be a unique addition of Ona people in Asmara area. Former signifies the diversification of the dietary habit. On the other hand, latter reflects one of the earliest adoptions of this Near Eastern staple in the Horn of Africa. (D'Andrea, et al. 2008).

We find considerable variations in food ways and animal husbandry across the Asmara plateau. Probably, it reflects a cultural adaptation to the different topography, climate, and soil condition. Some community ate domesticated small ungulates such as sheep and goats. In contrast, some others[10] consumed both the large[11] as well as small ungulates. It seems that the subsistence pattern of these Ona communities depended heavily on domestic animals such as cattle, sheep, goat, mammals, chickens, game birds, and antelopes. Highland region were also home to raptors, carnivores, and snakes during this period. The region may have enjoyed a savanna type vegetation or open woodlands in the mid first millennium BCE.[12] (Shoshani, et al. 2008).

There is amazing similarity in stone tools from Ancient Ona sites,[13] late Stone Age sites, Neolithic settlments, Pre-Aksumite sites, and Aksumite-period settlements. The ancient Ona people produced mainly flakes, scrapers, and baked tools (Figure 5.7 and Figure 5.8). This further indicates the existence of an agro-pastoral economy. We also find others tools such as burin, bi-faces, perforator, and points. Probably, these tools were used for harvesting and processing grains; cutting, scraping, and removing hair from skins; and fashioning clothes, bags, and other items.[14] Interestingly, there appears to be a broad similarity in terms of raw material, techno-typology, and context of the tools among these ancient Ona communities. As far as raw material is concerned, it mainly consists of quartz, chert, basalt, quartzite, and obsidian. All these raw materials except obsidian were available locally. Obsidian was perhaps imported from Red Sea area, where it was available in plenty. This shows trade relation between the ancient Ona people and population residing near Red Sea. Probably, these Ona people may have exchanged local products for obsidian. (Teka and Okubatsion 2008).

Figure 5.7: The stone tools (scraper, point, blade, and burin etc) from Mai Hutsa Ona site.

Figure 5.8: The stone artifacts from Ona Gudo site.

The society of these people appears to be relatively prosperous and egalitarian. There is very little sign of political or social differentiation. But towards their end, we do see some glimpses of differentiation in architecture and material culture. They also show some signs of growth of urbanism from the very early period. These communities developed an extensive network of gold mining. One of the important characteristic of these people was the location of large number of their communities near these gold mines. Agriculture, pastoralism, and gold mining gave rise to a diverse and complex population. These activities would have led to nucleation of populations. (Teka and Okubatsion 2008).

Probably, they possessed a common culture. There were commonalities in economy, architecture, and belief system. They manufactured small sculpture in the form of bull's head (Figure 5.9 and Figure 5.10).[15] It may be the product of young people during their initiation rituals. These bull heads are widely found across the central part of the Asmara basin between 700-500 BCE. They made images of cattle that also included depictions of *Bos indicus.* This

Figure 5.9: The stone bull head from Weki Duba Ona site.

Figure 5.10: The quartz bull heads from Mai Hutsa Ona site.

concrete evidence of their presence so early[16] has great significance. This animal has high milk producing capacity[17] and possesses natural resistance to disease. The relative predictability and stability associated with their milk production may have gone a long way in allowing the contemporary people have a sedentary life and progress towards urbanism. (Teka and Okubatsion 2008).

SIGNIFICANCE OF THE ANCIENT ONA SITES

Figure 5.11: The on-site museum at ancient Ona site of Sembel.

The ancient Ona sites unravel some vital mysteries about primordial complex human organization in Eritrea as well as Horn of Africa. It has helped in reconstructing the Eritrea's ancient history. These Ona sites hold great potential in economic terms for the local communities[18] as well as the larger national economy.[19] It could benefit the local community economically through tourism and involvement in formal educational programme and research activities.[20] It is also possible through building on-site museums on these Ona sites. This should be supplemented by development of near-site facilities such as craft sales, food services, and recreational infrastructure. Ancient Ona sites could bring significant economic benefits to this nation. It has immense potential to attract tourists from across the world.

In fact, most of these Ona sites are in and around Asmara. Latter being the capital city has most of the necessary infrastructure[21] to cater to the needs and service of tourists. There is a possibility of linking the Ona heritage sites with the amazing colonial architecture of Asmara for viable tourism in this area. The integration of ancient Ona heritage sites in the wider canvass of Eritrean tourism would lead to several benefits such as wider recognition of heritage sites as historical facts;[22] learning lessons from the past experiences for the continuity, survival, renewal and development of contemporary communities; creation and maintenance of unique cultural identity; facilitating public education; and providing leisure and recreational facilities.

The income from these on-site museums could be further used in sustaining the development, conservation, and management of these irreplaceable heritages. In fact, these ancient Ona sites faces considerable threats of destruction from various actors and factors such as expansion of agriculture, rapid urbanization, land distribution schemes, mismanagement of concerned institutions, and natural degradation and deterioration etc.[23] (Okubay 2008).

Thus, we can say that these ancient Ona communities holds a great promise for unraveling many of the enigmas associated with the early communities of Eritrea as well as Horn. Their existence belies or gives a severe jolt to the earlier argument that the genesis of Eritrean highlands people's culture lays in south Arabian Peninsula or the Nile Basin or the Ethio-Sabaean cultural complex.[24] It is based on limited architectural remains, specialized funerary ceramics, and epigraphic evidence. Ancient Ona communities do not seem to be influenced by the South Arabian incursions at least significantly on the basis of present evidences.

These communities also provide us the opportunity to explore the rapid incorporation of domesticated plants into pastoral adaptations. It also allows us a fresh perspective on prehistoric agricultural economy in the Horn of Africa.

These ancient Ona communities reflect how communities with many cultural affinities also differed across a landscape that was densely populated. In fact, we could say that these ancient Ona communities were agropastoral since the very early days of their occupation in the region. Moreover, there seems to be two distinct dietary zones in Asmara Basin in both crop and meat production and consumption. They had developed a very complex settlement and subsistence pattern. Ancient Ona communities had a very developed and efficient tool industry. These people also shared a common culture. The ancient Ona community sites are threatened by several forces. There is an urgent need for corrective measures to conserve and promote them in the best interest of posterity.

ENDNOTES

1. It was so especially in the highlands of Akele Guzai.
2. It refers to the area in and around Asmara.
3. The closer spacing is found in the cluster located in the northern part of the Greater Asmara area. It may be due to the presence of gold workings among these communities. In contrast, there seems to be wider spacing in the clusters located in the southern part of the area. This may be because of the fact that this area is situated on the edge of a productive plain. (Curtis, and Schmidt 2008).
4. It may be due to the fact that these rocks were unsuitable for agriculture.
5. This holds true even in present day Eritrea.
6. These activities may include baby caring, children tending, food preparing and eating, cattle feeding and watering, grain sweeping, chaff clearing, and grain bagging and transportation. (Curtis, and Schmidt 2008).
7. It marked the shift from pastoralism to agriculture in Horn of Africa.
8. It refers to bread wheat.
9. This seems to have happened towards the mid first millennium BCE.
10. It is especially true of Ona community living in Sembel, Sembel Kushet, and Ona Gudo sites.
11. It specifically refers to *Bos indicus* that flourished in this area during the Ona period.

12. It is reflected by the discovery of antelope in Mai Chiot site in Asmara. Antelope are generally found in savanna and open woodland areas.
13. It is true of Ona sites located in Greater Asmara area.
14. These items may have been made for personal and daily use.
15. It may have been derived from the reduction of large quartz blanks intended to produce ritual images of cattle. This seems to be especially true in case of Mai Hutsa site in Greater Asmara area.
16. It shows their presence in the beginning of first millennium BCE.
17. They have such capacity even under arid conditions.
18. Local community refers to part of the population residing in the vicinity of these sites.
19. It is because the benefit to the local community and tourism department would ultimately add to the larger national income.
20. The member of local communities could be employed as site administrators, site interpreters, and site guards. They could also be used as assistants and workers in archaeological explorations and excavations with some training.
21. It consists of several international hotels as well less expensive pensions, international airport, travel agencies, and tourism ministry and its outlets etc.
22. The Ancient Ona sites give us some insights besides others into the origin of life among contemporary highlander of Eritrea.
23. First of all, there is immediate need of conservation of these Ona sites.
24. It is based on limited architectural remains, specialized funerary ceramics, and epigraphic evidence. Ancient Ona communities do not seem to be influenced by the South Arabian incursions at least significantly on the basis of present evidences.

9

Adulite Era

Adulis was one of the most prominent trading ports in the ancient world. It was a renowned port city on the northeast African coast. Adulis had two satellite ports such as Samidi and Gabaza associated with it. It holds a very important position among the archaeological sites in Eritrea. Adulis's history begins in first millennium BCE from the Ptolemaic period and continues till the fall of the Aksumite kingdom in the late 1st millennium CE.

LOCATION

There is an ongoing scholarly debate upon the identification of ancient Adulis. Henry Salt was one of the pioneers[1] and identified the ruins on the plain of Zula as of Adulis. Casson argued for the modern port city of Massawa as the site of early Adulis. He also opined the shifting of the site from there to the plain of Zula at a later date. But, Salt's argument corresponds to the information provided by *Periplus.*

However, the present research shows that ancient Adulis is located near Afta and Zula villages in the Foro Sub Zone of Eritrea. It lies on the western seashores of the Red Sea coast about 4 km inland from the sea.[2] Adulis is situated about 50 kilometers south of present port city of Massawa. (Blue, et al. 2008). The Eritrean eastern escarpments and the Red Sea lie on the west and east of the Adulis respectively. Latter also shows it to be 15-20 meters above sea level. At present, the site is moderately covered by small bushes and sands.

SOURCE

Broadly speaking, there are two kinds of sources for the reconstruction of Adulite history. They are foreign accounts and archaeological sources. As far as the foreign accounts are concerned, the *Periplus of the Erythraean Sea*[3] and *The Christian Topography*[4] are most important ones. Besides that Adulis is also found in the biographies of a number of historians and travellers.

As far as archaeological sources are concerned, at least two surveys and four excavations have been carried out. The Adulis site was first surveyed by a French mission in 1840s. (Lefebvre 1845-49: Munro-Hay 1982). However, the first excavation was carried out by a British military engineer, William West Goodfellow in 1868. His team excavated three small test units and found ancient buildings and remains of material artifacts such as curved marble, marble capital, ceramics, and coins. Goodfellow also succeeded in excavating a Byzantine church at the south-east corner of the site. He was followed by another Briton, Theodore Bent. Bent surveyed the site and noted architectural similarities among the Adulis, Aksum, and Koloe.

In 1906, Richard Sundstrom excavated a substantial structure on the site. He referred to the excavated building as the 'royal palace.'[5] (Sundstrom 1907). Sundstrom excavation was followed by an Italian expedition led by Roberto Paribeni. Latter carried out substantial excavations at the south-west corner of Adulis, as well as at the site of two Byzantine churches. (Paribeni 1907). However, the last excavation was conducted by Francois Anfray in the early 1960s.

The most latest archaeological survey was conducted by an Eritro-British expedition in 2004-05. The team consisted of the members from the Universities of Asmara and Southampton, the National Museum of Eritrea, and the Northern Red Sea Regional Museum in Massawa. This archaeological team achieved resounding success by establishing a chronology for the growth and development of Adulis, reconstruction of its settlement pattern,[6] and identification of the ports of the *Periplus*[7] and Cosmos.[8]

ETYMOLOGY

During the period of Pharaohs,[9] the ancient Egyptians knew it with the name of *Outoulit.* According to Pliny the Elder, Adulis meant a place founded by escaped Egyptian slaves.[10] Therefore, sometimes Adulis is called as "the city of free people." Ancient geographers have mentioned Adulis as a big thriving port in their account. Not surprisingly, early people also called it as the "Berenice of Sabaeans."[11] Adulis was originally the center of a local population known as Adulitae. (Munro-Hay 1989). According to some scholars, Adulis derived its name from the ancient name of the village Azulli. The pre-Islamic Arabs called it *Aduli.* Interestingly, the ships made there were called Adulite. According to the anonymous author of the *Periplus of the Erythraean Sea,* Adulis was a fair sized village about 20 stades (3.3 km) from the sea. However, according to the present inhabitants of the area, the Saho ethnic group, *Adolos* means white water, referring to 'white coloured water' of the seashore.[12]

POLITY

As already mentioned, the history of Adulis goes back to thousands of years. According to one view, since Adulis was known to ancient Egyptian, it may have formed the part of the "Land of Punt." In fact, the lower strata of Adulis site are dated from the middle of the 2nd millennium BCE to the early millennium BCE. The Greek and Phoenician ships frequently visited Adulis around 7th century BCE.

According to one view, it was founded by the Ptolemy's. In the mid 3rd century BCE, Ptolemy II Philadelphus[13] established it as a port. Cosmas[14] described two inscriptions indicating the territorial claims of two different monarchs such as Ptolemy III Euergetes of Egypt (246-221 BCE) and an unknown Adulitic or Aksumitic king. (Kirwan 1972). So, a Ptolemaic Egypt could not be ruled out. The port city seemed to have been developed during the time of Ptolemy Euergetes. It began to serve large ships in the middle of the 3rd century BCE. Some potsherds recovered from the Adulis site date from the Augustan period through to the 1st century CE.

One of the excavations in Adulis[15] revealed the ruins of a temple which seemed to be Greek in structure and architecture. This temple probably dates back to the pre-Roman age when the Greeks settled in this port city. This archeological mission ascertains without doubt that there was life in Adulis before the Ptolemaic period. They also found type of ceramic[16] widely believed to have been produced indigenously. However, when the Romans established their hegemony in the region, Adulis relation shifted from Greeks towards them.

Adulis seemed to have played an important role in the development of city-states like Qohaito, Matara, Keskese, Tokenda'e, Dera'a, Yaha, and Hawelte etc, in Eritrea in early Common Era. These city states were formed and developed due to their linkages with Adulis. Later on, they became part of the Aksumite kingdom. Probably, Adulis enjoyed a separate, autonomous, and tribute paying status at this time.

It seems that Adulis was incorporated by the Aksumite Empire with the passage of time. The author of the *Periplus of the Erythraean Sea* mentions Zoscales as the ruler of the region. Probably, he was an early king of Aksum. (Munro-Hay 1989b). From the 2nd to the 6th century CE, Adulis enjoyed its luxurious period during the reigns of Kings Ezana and Kaleb and became one of the three famous ports[17] in the Read Sea coast. *Periplus* further mentioned about "the city of Axomite" through which the majority of the ivory traded at Adulis was transported.

It also seems that Adulis served as a base for the Aksumite expansion to south Arabia.[18] Undoubtedly, Adulis was as vital to Aksum as Aksum to Adulis. Some scholars have also proposed the possibility of Adulis being a center of an independent state during this time. (Blue, et al. 2008). According to Adulis inscription some of the people who were invaded by a anonymous king were Agame (Eastern Tigray), Gaz (Agazian), Aua (Adwa-Adi-Aua), Tekeze, Samene, Lazine, Zaa, Gabala (Mensa and Habab), Beja (Beni Amir),

Arabitas (Arabs), and Land of the Sabeans (The Sabean Kingdom) etc.

However, Adulis declined with the decay of Aksumite kingdom. The Red Sea fell under the hegemony of the Persians, the new ruler of south Arabia after the Aksumite defeat at their hands. Persians established their control over Adulis and the Dahlak Islands. This contributed in blocking Roman and other trade traffic to Adulis. It became an abandoned city and lost its historic role. Some scholars believed that Adulis was razed by an Arab expedition of 640 CE led by Umar ibn-al Khattab. (Budge 1928; Hourani 1951; Munro-Hay 1982). However, finally it was laid to ruins by the Bejas raids.[19] The site seemed to have been completely destroyed. There are no upstanding remains. The evidence of a fierce burning is prevalent in its ruins. This indicates the death knell of one of the most important port city of the antiquity.

The numismatic evidence from the site seemed to suggest its continued occupation till 7th century CE. It is plausible that a political shift took place in the southern Red Sea region with the rise of Islam combined with the decline in Byzantine trade. These development forced Aksumite kingdom to look inward. According to Munro-Hay, the Aksum and Adulis certainly lost its influence in region by early 8th century CE, when the Arab Abd al-Malik occupied the Dahlak Island to counter the piracy. (Munro-Hay 1982). Some scholars believe the natural disasters like flooding and earthquake being responsible for its decline.

ECONOMY

Adulis connected the hinterland with ancient Egypt, Roman and Greek empires, and also probably China and India through trade via the Red Sea. The archaeological evidences of Adulite goods have been found from Egypt to India. (Peacock, et al. 2006; Tomber 2005). It exported tortoise shell, ivory, horn, obsidian, and slaves. Adulis imported cloth, fabric, brass, glass, copper, coinage, wine, olive oil, and jewellery. (Munro Hay 1982). Possibly, they also exported wild animals like elephants and rhinoceroses and gold acquired from the Eritrean hinterland. (Blue, et al. 2008).

The Adulite had commercial relations with the ancient Egyptians. They exchanged animals, minerals, precious woods, and incense with Egyptian ornaments, armaments, and tools. With the fall of Egypt in the hands of the Ptolemies, Adulite commercial relation extended as far as Greek. The Arab merchants were forced to leave the Red Sea to their powerful rival, the Greeks and shift their way towards Syria. The Greeks under Ptolemy III enlarged Adulis as one of the important historic station.

In Roman period, Adulis was the most important entrepot on the coast of northeast Africa south of Egypt. It enjoyed thriving commercial relation with the Romans. Adulis became a key port of the Romans for their eastern trade. The fourteen Roman gold coins found in Matara attest to the strong trade relationship between Adulis and the Romans. Archaeologists have also found the evidence of late Roman amphorae at the Adulis site dated to at least late 5th to early 6th centuries. Moreover, large quantities of potteries have been discovered from this site dating to 10 BCE-150 CE or 260 CE. (Blue, et al. 2008). Adulis was filled with the Greco-Roman products during the Ptolemaic, Roman, and the early Byzantine ages. These goods moved to the interior land from there. Cosmas described Adulis as a very prosperous commercial center repeatedly visited by Greeks and Romans from the Elanitic Gulf and Alexandria.

The Chinese also had trade relation with Adulis. They acquired rhinoceros, its horn, turtle shell, and ivory from here. Some scholars believed that Adulis particularly had commercial relations with the Han dynasty of China.[20] The contemporary writers mentioned that the Chinese under latter's rule had some commercial relation with the African coast of the Red Sea, which was referred as Hwang Chi. Perhaps, latter was the Aksumite kingdom that utilized Adulis as the gateway to conduct its outside trade via the Sea. Adulis played a role of leading port in the Aksumite kingdom especially in promoting latter's commercial relationship with outside world. In fact, a large chunk of Aksum's external trade was conducted through Adulis.

Adulis served as a bridge for the trade between east and west. It has been mentioned for its contact with India, Persia, and Yemen. Adulis functioned as an intermediary trading station where the big ships coming from India, the Persian Gulf, and east Africa exchanged goods such as wheat, rice, sesame, cotton, cloth, and honey with the vessels coming from Egypt and the Arabian Peninsula. Its importance further grew with the discovery of seaway to India.[21]

Adulite imported emeralds from the Bejas and sold it to India. It seems that the Arabs used this natural port for their commercial contact with the African coasts. The Mediterranean and the Arabic Peninsula's amphorae have been discovered from the site. Adulis seemed to have become a pre-eminent port of northeast Africa by 4th-5th century CE. Its dock used to be filled with ships from Egypt, Arabian Peninsula, India, and Ceylon. (Kirwan 1972). The discovery of imported Mediterranean amphorae and eastern Sigillata[22] in Adulis, Egypt, and India in the 1st century context further reinforces the centrality of Adulis in antique trading networks.

Several ancient writers have attested to the greatness of Adulite civilization. Pliny described Adulis as a very large commercial port, for both the Trogodolytes (the people of the coast) and Aksumite (people of the mountain plateau). The author of *Periplus of the Erythraean Sea* mentioned Adulis as a great port city and a commercial center exporting ivory, rhinoceros horns, skins, gold, myrrh, frankincense, tortoise shell, hippopotamus and elephant's hide, cassia, cinnamon, slaves, apes, and elephants. It imported items such as unfurled cloths, arsinoitic robes, cloaks, linen, several sorts of glass wares, used ornaments, cooking pots, armlets, anklets, iron used for spear, axe, adze, swords, sups of bronze, money, wine, oil, garments, silver, and gold objects etc. Adulis established itself as the most important commercial port in the Red Sea by 1st century CE. According to the author of the *Periplus of the Erythrean Sea*:

> "It was a thriving organized society living in a big city of beautiful buildings, temples, baths and wide streets. Big ships from the Arabian ocean brought its daggers, spears, glass and sailed from it laden with ivory, rhinoceros horn and turtle skins."

This statement amply reflects the greatness of Adulis as a great port city in it's hey days and as a major business center with vast architectural foundation. This important port city also features prominently in the 6th century *Christian Topography.* It has also been referred to as "a legally limited port." One scholar has interpreted it as a place where trade was limited and controlled by a ruler rather than being a free bazaar. (Casson 1989).

SOCIETY AND CULTURE

It seems that Adulis was a large city covering some 38 hectares. The city seems to be un-walled.[23] Latter may indicate the presence of a central authority capable of ensuring the security of an economically vital region. The city saw massive growth during 1st-6th century. The remains of building indicate high level achievement of the city. Several artifacts such as curved marble columns, depicted figures on marble slabs, rotational and circular grinding stones, amphora wares; and varieties of ceramics including clay pots, glassware, and coins indicates the practice of various arts and crafts.

Adulite communities seemed to be distinct from the hinterland people. They practiced fishing. Probably, it constituted an important part of their dietary habits. Camel seemed to have been used as the beast of the burden. There are several evidences of Adulites cultural and belief system. Paribeni uncovered a semi-circular apse structure called the altar of the sun. It indicates towards a religious basilica church. He also found baptismal tank and remains of eight pillars arranged octagonally.

Adulis served as the melting pot for the oriental and occidental culture as it functioned as the meeting point of traders of both the region. Adulis was in close contact and in turn influenced by Greeks, Phoenicians, Romans, Egyptian, Arabian, and Indian cultures. Not surprisingly, they were referred to as "the people of the coast." One of its probable king Zoscales is known as "the ruler of the coast." He is said to be well versed in Greek literature. This indicates the Greek influence in Adulis area.

The Greeks exercised huge influence upon Adulis in terms of culture and artistic style. This was possible due to long thriving trade between the two. The Greek writing system spread along Adulis and nearby areas. Its evidence in the form of inscription in Greek script on several monuments has been found in Adulis as well as from several places along the Red Sea coast and the interior of Eritrea (Decemhare and Dembezan). The buildings in Adulis and Qohaito further indicate the influence of Greek art and Architecture. Furthermore, Greek coins have been found in Adulis as well as several places on the coast of Red Sea. The Greek culture spread to Aksumite kingdom with the latter's occupation of Adulis.

Although the Adulite people could not set up a distinct kingdom, they had a remarkable civilization that was mainly characterized by commercial relation with other contemporary civilizations of the ancient world such as Egyptian, Greek, Roman, and Aksum. The city experienced a scattered and relatively unplanned growth in its earliest phase. However, later the city seemed to have been built according to a regulated grid plan.

Throughout the Aksumite period, Adulis served the kingdom as the main outlet for its external trade relations. The Aksumite kingdom could not have achieved its hegemony and fame[24] without using Adulis as a center of its commerce since its trade relations played outstanding role in strengthening the kingdom. It also played crucial role in the rise and fall of contiguous city-states and kingdoms.[25] In fact, the port became a great depot for the goods coming from across the world. It seems that Adulis played a major role as a trading center connecting several regions. Moreover, it also served as an important gateway through which new objects and ideas were passed. Adulis not only contributed as the center of trade items but also the ideas, believes, technology, and other social systems.

ENDNOTES

1. He tried to identify it in early 19th century (1814).
2. But according to another account, at present Adulis lies 7 km away from the sea although it is referred as the ancient port city. This indicates the possibility of major coastal change since antiquity.
3. It was a guide book for the Greco-Roman merchants of the 1st century CE.
4. It was written anonymously in the 6th century CE by an Alexandrian monk, later given the pseudonym Cosmos Indicopleustes or Indian Voyager. (Kirwan 1972).
5. This interpretation has been contested by other archaeologists.
6. It has been able to reconstruct the building layout of the ancient city and gain a greater understanding of its size and extent in the later Aksumite period.
7. A small fossil seastack (173 m × 35 m) of the eastern end of the Galala hills has been identified as the location of Diodorus Island. The Deseas Oriene has been identified as the hilly island of the Periplus.
8. Cosmos marked a site north of the Adulis as Samidi. The Eritro-German expedition identified it with the two mound of schist separated by 500 m.
9. It refers to Middle Kingdom of Ancient Egypt, c.1450 CE. (Soni 2007).
10. According to Pliny, it was founded by fugitive slaves fleeing from their Egyptian lords.
11. The Egyptian port of Bernice was very famous at that time.
12. Perhaps, it results from the splash of the wave or water current.
13. He was one of the Greek Ptolemy kings who ruled Egypt after the disintegration of the Alexander's Empire.
14. He was an ancient writer of the 5th century CE.

15. This excavation was undertaken by the Italian mission headed by Paribeni and Gallina in 1906.
16. This type of ceramic is found in the deeper and oldest layer of the soil (about 10 meters below the top soil). These ceramics are decorated with graphite and simple as well as complex designs. They are also decorated with horizontal lines and geometrical shapes such as triangles, zigzags, semicircles; or broken, winding, and wavy lines.
17. The other two were Mouza and Obollah.
18. The Aksumite kingdom was able to establish its power over it for some period.
19. It probably happened in the years between 630 and 640 CE.
20. It flourished between 220-589 CE.
21. Greeks discovered the sea way to India.
22. It is a type of ceramic wares.
23. Paribeni voiced the same opinion in 1907. This has been further confirmed by the Erito-British archaeological expedition of Adulis. According to Munro-Hay, non-fortification is a common feature of several Aksumite settlements of the similar period.
24. It was counted among the four contemporary great kingdoms of the ancient world.
25. The kingdom here refers to Aksum and Meroe.

10

Aksumite Period

Generally Eritrean sees Aksum civilization as an Ethiopian historical and cultural heritage. But, it is a misconception. Both Eritrea and Ethiopia has contributed to the rise and progress of this ancient civilization. In fact, any part of erstwhile Aksumite Empire may envy the extremely rich Aksumite cultural remains in present southern Eritrea. The settlement and other evidences related to this great civilization abounds in places like Qohaito, Adikeih, Matara, Hishmele, Keskese, and Ham etc. Here, an attempt has been made to systematically explore and analyze their contribution and influences in Aksumite civilization.

The term "Aksumite" has ancient origin. It was used by several ancient travellers and geographers. The *Periplus of the Erythraean Sea* used this term in 1st century CE to denote a powerful cultural group in northern highlands that had developed a metropolis and engaged in international trade. Ptolemy referred to Aksum as the royal capital. The Aksumite period extended from150 BCE-700 CE. This phase is characterized by political, economic, and socio-cultural complexity and state civilization centered in the highlands of Eritrea and northern Ethiopia.

AKSUMITE CULTURE

Aksumite culture seemed to have developed from the preceding "Pre-Aksumite" and "Proto-Aksumite" cultures. There is also broad unanimity among scholars over its African origin. Aksumite state was successful in expanding the northern Horn's influence in a large area. It succeeded in reorganizing its relationship with Romans and Byzantine by 1st CE. It also established relationship with India, Persia, Syria, and Sri Lanka. (Desanges 1969; Mordini 1960; Munro-Hay 1996; Pankhurst 1974; Wolska-Conus 1968-73).

The Aksumite state had developed urban centers, monetary structure,[1] an intensive agricultural system, and a powerful military by 4th century CE. It also adopted Christianity during this period that went on to develop and expand over next two centuries. In fact, Christianity was firmly established by 6th century CE, and played an important role in its relation with Romans and Byzantines.

However, this state became a full-fledged empire between 4th-6th centuries. It followed an expansionist policy in northern Horn and southern Red Sea regions. There are evidences of Aksumite settlements in north-eastern and north-western Tigray, Ethiopia, Akele Guzai region, Rora region,[2] area south of the Takkezze River, along the Eritrean Red Sea coast,[3] and beside an axis stretching from Aksum to the Gulf of Zula. (Anfray 1967; Anfray and Annequin 1965; Fattovich, et al. 2000; Munro-Hay 1991; Phillipson 1998, 2000). The Aksumite state controlled important trade routes and established commercial links with Nubia, Egypt, Syria, and several African and Indian Ocean states and communities. (Fattovich, et al. 2000; Kobishchanov 1979, 1981; Mordini 1960; Munro-Hay 1989b, 1991, 1996; Phillipson 1998, 2000).

The Aksumite settlements were characterized by expansive residential areas consisting of commoner, middle-rank, and elite houses with diversity in function and form. (Anfray 1967; Anfray and Annequin 1965; Fattovich, et al. 2000; Munro-Hay 1991; Phillipson 1998, 2000). The urban centers were closely linked to hinterlands that produced extensive area of settlement and high population density. Its architectural features included the multi-story buildings, dressed stone elements, architectural and agricultural terraces and platforms, complex shafts, multi-chamber tombs, and monumental stone stelae. (Buxton and Matthews 1974; Littmann, et al. 1913; Phillipson 1997, 1998, 2000; Philliposn and Reynolds 1996; Plant 1978). Another important feature was a complex agricultural system involving terracing, plough farming, irrigation, and dam. The Aksumite settlements were able to produce food that allowed and sustained urban and rural populations and demographic complexity.

QOHAITO, ADIKEIH, KESKESE, AND THEIR HINTERLAND

Qohaito[4] was one of the major ancient metropolis and an important destination in trade between Adulis and Aksum. It is strategically located along an axis of settlements stretching from north-central Tigray to the Gulf of Zula. Qohaito represents a plethora of single as well as clusters of sites spread out over much of the Qohaito plateau.[5] These historical remains are placed on top of the Qohaito plateau. Its ancient ruins are located in the historical province of Akele Guzai. At present, it comes under Zoba Dabub administrative zone. Qohaito is 32 square kilometers in area. It lies 2600 meters above sea level. Qohaito is approximately 15 kilometers east of Adikeih, and 32 kilometers west of the Red Sea coast. The plateau receives around 500-700 millimeters rainfall annually. As far as vegetation is concerned, it consists of juniper trees; acacia species; aloe;[6] evergreen and semi-evergreen bush land and thicket;[7] and some montane[8] forests.

There are literary as well as archaeological sources for the study of Qohaito and Aikeih historical area. Some scholars identify Qohaito as the ancient market city of Koloe. (Bent 1896; Munro-Hay 1991; Phillipson 1998). Koloe has been mentioned by Ptolemy as an interior town and the first major settlement on the route from Adulis to Aksum. *The Periplus of the Erythraean Sea* also refers to Koloe as an inland town, a three-day journey from Adulis and five days from Aksum. (Casson 1989; Huntingford 1980). In 2nd century CE, the

Alexandrian geographer, Claudius Ptolomaeus wrote about another town known as Maste. Some historians believe that it might represent any of the four ancient towns such as Qohaito, Matara, Keskese, and Der'a. Aue is still another ancient town to be identified with Qohaito. It has been mentioned by ambassador of the Byzantine Emperor, Justinian Nonnosus around 533 CE. According to him, Aue was situated between Adulis and Aksum. (Bent 1896).

Qohaito's historical remains spread over an area of 68 square kilometers.[9] It consists of several mounds,[10] mound complexes, town ruins, monumental structures, dams, basins, necropolis, tombs, watch towers, individual building structures, wall features, kilns, small and large dwellings, paved roads, rock engravings and inscriptions (Figure 6), stele, open air prayer areas, lithic artifacts, and ceramics. The major archaeological attractions are monumental platforms marked by pillars, the dam, and the rock hewn shaft tomb. The immediate surrounding contains dense rock art.

Figure 6: South Arabian inscriptions at Awalu Ghalba north of the Qohaito plateau.

On the basis of present research,[11] much of the sites on Qohaito plateau could be dated to Aksumite period. The ceramic evidence includes Aksumite potsherds. These comprises of red ware, black ware, and cream-coloured amphorae.

One of the important archaeological sites in Qohaito area is ORz01.[12] It represents the remains of a monumental podium that consist of a platform with pillars. The podium measures almost 9.30 × 11.80 meters. It sits on a bedrock surface and contains five rebated layers reaching 0.5 meter in height. The rooms at the four corner of the building measures 2.20 × 2.20 meters. It is interesting to note that there is sandstone masonry done. Perhaps, podium may have been bearing plastered face during the Aksumite period. The four sandstone pillars on the podium include stepped-shaped capitals. Probably in all likely hoods, it must have supported wooden beams. The building has an entrance on the eastern side. It seems to have had a slate floor. The ORz01 podium and pillared building seems to fit in the general frame work of elite Aksumite architecture.

There are indications of the existence of several ancient dams in the area. But today, only the dam of Safira[13] exists. (Libsekal 2008). Perhaps, this dam was made in mid 1st millennium BCE. It is mainly built of large blocks of stones. In fact, this area hosts the highest concentration of sites on Qohaito plateau.[14] Safira area has large concentration of ancient small sized houses with narrow streets. This might represent the non-elite area.

There are several temple-like structures just southeast of Safira dam. It consists of cisterns, well-spaced streets, and large dwellings. These structures are built on podium with pillars. This could have been the elite residential area. There is an underground tomb located east of this elite area. This tomb is referred to as 'Egyptian tomb' and probably belongs to Common Era. Another significant structure is a large walled enclosure. It might be the remains of a market area or a caravan resting place. The walls branch in several directions and might have lined ancient roadways.

The buildings are mostly made from cream-grey-coloured sandstone. Whereas, the other architectural features such as dressed corner blocks, water-piping features, and other architectural blocks are made up of a harder and darker variety of sandstone. The red bricks are also seen in at least one mound features. Slate is also scattered throughout the area.

The modern settlements near these sites show continuity in several ways. The variety and sizes of chisel cut marks on the pillars and corner stone indicate the existence of once locally made tools. The kiln like structure at the eastern edge of the plateau could have been a "*Mahgoda*" area, an ancient traditional technique of iron melting in Eritrean region.[15]

Adikeih plateau is located almost 2 kilometers west of the Qohaito plateau. In an archaeological exploration, 27 ancient mounds[16] were discovered. The surveys have exposed the prominent mound features with architectural rubble and the ruins of an ancient building. One observes similarities in mound composition, architectural elements, and ceramic traditions among the Qohaito and its hinterland sites.[17] This might indicate the existence of a common cultural system in the past. However, one finds diversity in mound size and placement. This might show specialization and interdependence among hinterland communities. There exist at least three large sites that are strategically located on the plateau periphery overlooking adjacent canyon and valley.[18] A number of rock shelter sites[19] containing rock art are in abundance in the immediate Qohaito hinterland.[20] One also finds south Arabian inscriptions at some sites such as Awalu Ghalba.

The Hishmele area is located near the northwestern edge of the Adikeih plateau. It is approximately 2 km from the present Adikeih town. Its major archaeological attractions are mound features, rock paintings,[21] architectural rubble, remnant of an ancient building, and scattered potsherds. One building found in the area dates back to

Aksumite period. It is roughly rectangular in shape and made up of closely fitted stones.

Qohaito represents a complex ancient metropolis with a diverse range of functions. Probably, it performed the functions of both a political and a market center. Overall, Qohaito represents an ancient urban city surrounded by many towns and hamlets. It seems to have been one of the largest ancient settlements linked to an expansive hinterland in Aksumite period. Adikeih sites are the concrete evidence of extensive urban hinterland around Qohaito and rivaling the density of ancient settlement surrounding the ancient Aksum. (Fattovich, et al. 2000; Michels 1994). It probably owed its prosperity to caravan trade between Adulis and Aksum. Qohaito linked the Aksumite capital to the ancient port city of Adulis and the Gulf of Zula via the Komaile and Haddas valleys. If it was the ancient Koloe then undoubtedly, it was more than a market center.

MATARA

One of the largest and important Aksumite settlements was Matara. Matara[22] is situated 1 kilometer south of present town of Senafe in the central highlands of the southern Akele Guzai region of Eritrea. As already mentioned, it belongs to both "Pre-Aksumite" as well as Aksumite periods. As far as the Aksumite period evidences are concerned, at least 161 coins with depictions of 8 Aksumite emperors[23] were recovered. A bronze lamp of Hellenistic style has also been found. The Aksumite period occupation in Matara has been divided into two phases such as pre-Christian period (100-500 CE) and Christian period (600-800 CE). The site contains "elite villa" residences,[24] commoner buildings, and churches. The stela of Matara was erected in 3rd century CE (Figure 6.2).[25] Archeologists have also discovered 3 rectangular-shaped church or church-like structures.[26] Stone tomb features have been found on the site.[27] Another area contains six simple stones and earthen tombs with stone slab roofs with osteological remains.

Figure 6.1: Author (Third from left) along with faculty members of Adikeih College of Arts and Social Sciences of Eritrea at Matara site.

Figure 6.2: The Matara Stela including an engraved disk, crescent symbol, and a four-line inscription in early Geez or proto-Geez.

Figure 6.3: The ruins of Matara site.

Figure 6.4: Aksumite period architecture at Matara showing finely dressed wall.

Four large structures on the site resembles the "elite palace" structure of Aksum. (Chittick 1974, 1976; Littmann, et al. 1913; Munro-Hay 1989a; Phillipson 1997, 1998). These structures possess conventional Aksumite architectural designs. Two residential quarters of densely packed contiguous stone and mud mortar dwellings with number of hearths and brick ovens have also been excavated. (Anfray 1967, 1974). These have been interpreted as "commoner residence." All these indicate the prevalence of social hierarchy at Matara. (Anfray 1974, 1981). This site also contains special use areas such as stables and workshops etc. There was once a plethora of rock cut tombs on an adjacent hill.[28] Other rock cut tombs were located on a hill to the north of the site. There are multiple sites in the areas surrounding Matara, interpreted as ancient farmstead. (Anfray 1967; Anfray and Annequin 1965).

KESKESE

Another large and an important Aksumite settlement was Keskese. It is located north of Matara and near the base of Amba Terica and the beginning point of Komaile valley directly linking the highlands with Adulis on the Red Sea littoral. This ancient settlement lies in highland valley near the edge of eastern escarpment. It is almost 2000 meters above sea level. Interestingly, Keskese is placed between the two important ancient urban centers of Matara and Qohaito.

Figure 6.5: Fragments of one of the fallen and broken square pillars in Keskese. The inscription includes a south Arabian name.

HAM

Ham is located in the Shimezana region of the Akele Guzai highlands. It is approximately 20 kilometers south-west of the present town of Senafe near the border with Tigray. Ham area contains a number of archaeological and historical sites of the Aksumite culture period including those in and around the Christian sanctuaries of Debra Libanos and Enda Maryam. According to local tradition, the Church Debra Libanos was built by a Syrian missionary, Abba Mata[29] during the late 5th or early 6th century CE. It is one of the oldest dating monastery and church in the Horn of Africa. (Buxton 1947; Tamrat 1972). Debra Libanos was originally located in the village Ham, but later on moved to a cliff adjacent to the Ham plateau. The Church possess a metal covered Bible containing copies of early 13th century CE land charters mentioning the Zagwe king Lalibela. (Rossini 1901, 1990).

The current church of Enda Maryam at Ham incorporates ancient architectural elements as well as Aksumite period artifacts, including monolithic pillars, a large stone basin, amphorae ceramic vessels, and a funerary inscription written in Geez. (Anfray 1965; Monneret de Villard 1940). One also finds ancient rock engravings of crosses, human and animal figures, multiple stone tumuli, and a possible fruit or oil press with three tanks and conduits carved into rock. (Anfray 1965). At least, 60 wrapped and desiccated ancient human bodies were uncovered from burials near Ham.

There are other contemporary archaeological sites in Akele Guzai region such as Gura, Afalba, Corbaria, and Dera in northern part; May Turub, Grat Mah Dere, Menah, Safra, Salham Nahara, Yegela, and Zeban Kuture in central Akele Guzai; Bet Abba Hanni, Dibdib, Aguadu, Edit,[30] Bihat, Guna Guna, Zala Kesad May, Ambesset, Zokollo, and Zala Bet Meka etc.

The great Aksumite civilization began declining by 7th century CE. Thus obviously the decay set in the thriving Aksumite communities at Qohaito, Adikeih, and Matara etc. There are several reasons attributed for its demise. Some scholars believed that it declined due to environmental degradation caused by overexploitation of resources. Others argued in terms of changes in international trading patterns in the Red Sea area and north-eastern Africa subsequent to Muslim expansion. (Bard, et. al. 2000; Butzer 1981; Fattovich, et al. 2000; Munro-Hay 1991; Phillipson 1998). It was also struck by plague and famine in the 536 CE. (Schmidt 2002b).

So, the numerous Aksumite period settlements in area like Qohaito, Adikeih, Matara, Hishmele, Keskese, and Ham etc., made tremendous contribution to rise and growth of Aksum civilization. They reflect the process of urban-hinterland and inter-regional relation and their interaction to the development of the ancient complex society. Undoubtedly, like Harappan civilization in Indian Subcontinent, Aksum civilization is not the exclusive heritage of either Eritrea or Ethiopia. Both the nations and their people should be proud of such a rich and glorious common past and heritage.

ENDNOTES

1. It brought in use currency that was struck in gold, silver, and copper.
2. It lies in the northern part of Eritrea.
3. It is especially found near the Gulf of Zula.
4. It is also called as Kohaito or Qohayto.
5. In 1996 and 1997, the German Archaeological Mission to Eritrea recorded and located over 900 archaeological sites on Qohaito plateau. It included at least 20 ancient "town ruins," 35 podium buildings, 15 cisterns, five rock inscription locations with Geez or Tigrinya Ethiopic script, and 15 loci with rock and engravings. The team was led by Steffen Wenig from Humboldt University in Berlin. (Eigner 1998, 1999; Kruger and Pospis 1997; Wenig 1997, 2003, 2006; Wolf 1997).
6. Aloe is a plant with fleshy toothed leaves and considered to be native to South Africa.
7. It refers to thick growth of bush.
8. It indicates forest belonging to mountainous regions.

9. It is 17 km by 4 km.
10. The mounds vary in size from 30 to 600 square meters.
11. The type of architecture, ceramic materials, and Geez inscriptions indicates towards Aksumite period occupations.
12. This site was mapped and documented by the German Archaeological Mission during their 1996 field work.
13. This dam is 67 meters long and almost 3 meters high at its center.
14. Probably, the reason is general scarcity of water on the plateau and relative abundance in Safira area.
15. It is still practiced in Der'a around Adikeih and at Tera-Emni, a village situated near the town of Mendefera.
16. It included the important Hishmele area.
17. The seven mound sites contained wall features of stone masonry similar in design and structure to those found at Qohaito and Matara.
18. These include the Haddas valley and the Rubba Himberten canyon. There are some large sites of Awalu Guda, Hitseyto, and Kinto that are located in the canyon and various *ambas* between Qohaito and Adikeih.
19. It includes sites such as Adi Alewti, Awalu Ghalba, Daqanamo, Emba Qalay, Emba Talba, Hishmele, Gao, Saro, Sehillo, and Engula.
20. A number of these sites contain large earthen floors. They could prove to be key sites in examining diachronic aspects of socio-political and economic change in the Qohaito area.
21. As far as the rock paintings are concerned, they are found in two rock shelters. The first one contains at least 17 humpless cattle figures and a row of seven human figures. They are painted in red colour. The second rock shelter contains at least one human figure, a series of black-coloured bovid figures, and a possible elephant figure. These paintings are similar to Sorre Hanakiya and early Dahthami stages of the Ethiopian-Arabian style of rock art. They possibly date to 3rd-1st millennium BCE. (Brandt and Carder 1987; Cervicek 1976: Negash 1997).
22. It is also known as Metera. The local inhabitants of the area call it Belew-Kelew.
23. It ranges in time from the reign of Emperor Afilas to Emperor Armah.
24. Anfray designated it as "elite villa."

25. It includes an engraved disk and crescent symbol and four line inscriptions in an early Geez or "Proto-Geez" script. The crescent symbol is often associated with the moon God Almaqah of south Arabia. The inscription reads "This is the stela which Agaz has made for his ancestors for their defeat of the forces of Asa Alefe and Tsebelen."
26. It might be dated from 5th-7th century CE.
27. One of them contains a funerary chapel and is 15 meters by 10 meters. (Anfray 1967).
28. This is Gwal Saim hill standing immediately to the east of the site.
29. It is also known as "Libanos."
30. It lies near Matara.

11

Post-Aksumite Period

8th century heralded the development of post-Aksumite Eritrea with the elements of both changes and continuity. Between the 8th and 13th centuries, a number of remarkable events took place such as disintegration of the great Aksumite kingdom, rise of Bejas, vast population migration, and spread of Islam in Eritrean region. The Bejas, a Cushitic people began making incursions into Aksumite territory along the sea coast and in the highlands of northwestern Eritrea, as early as the 4th century.

THE ORIGIN, RISE, AND EXPANSION OF THE BEJAS

Historically, the Bejas are believed to be a sub-division of eastern Cushitic people and well known for their expansion. They originated in Egyptian-Sudanese border areas[1] and lived between the Nile valley and the Red Sea since 2500 BCE. Bejas were forced to migrate from their homeland towards the south and west due to relative deficiency of the territory, Arab expansion, and conquest of the North Africa especially Egypt. They constantly moved south and westward. However during this migration, Bejas ran over the fertile lands along the Nile and spilled over into the Ethiopian deserts.

But very soon, they climbed the highlands where food and pasture were abundan (Kotler 1966). Bejas settled in central and eastern Sudan by 3rd century CE. First of all, they built the Blemmy state which was destroyed by Silko King of Nubia in the 6th century CE. From the very beginning, Bejas were disrupting trade routes in northern and southern Sudan. Towards the end of 7th century, the Zanafadj tribe moved up the Barka valley into Seraye. From that point onwards Beja expanded across the Eritrean plateau. (Killion 1998). Thereafter, they conquered the region west of Axum and marched into the northern most highlands of Eritrea, apparently seizing and perhaps destroying the Christian culture and forcing the inhabitants to flee southward. By the 9th century, Bejas seem to have occupied the main Aksumite centers of Akkele Guzai and the coastal plain of Semhar.

The relationship between Bejas and Aksumite was based on raids and counter raids. As the Aksumite sources indicate, the Bejas were the target of Ezana's military expeditions. However, the Bejas were responsible for severe blow to the Aksumites. They also destroyed the port of Adulis. (Sabby 1974). The Bejas established themselves in area extending from the Red Sea coast to the eastern part of Sudan after the collapse of Aksumite kingdom. They set up five different kingdoms such as Baqlin, Bazin, Jarin, Naqis, and Qata (Trimingham). Several of them contain names clearly related to modern Eritrean peoples and regions, including Hedareb, Manasa (Mensa), Baqlin (Baqla), and Bazin (Baza) etc. But Yaqubi, the geographer of the 19th century, claimed to have seen and recorded six Beja states.

The Beja's expansion and conquest in Eritrea covered the whole coastal areas north of Hergigo, the Sahel high plains, the Barka and Anseba valleys, as well as most of the highlands. They fought against the pre-existing population for supremacy. Probably, the exiting population was subjugated. In the 8th century, Bejas invaded the Barka valley and the slopes of Eritrean plateau and conquered parts of the province of Hamassien and the coastal plains. The Bejas settled in Massawa about mid 8th century with the purpose of occupying the Red Sea coasts. Bejas deep penetration is attested by their graves in the Eritrean plateau.

THE BEJA KINGDOMS

The Bejas unified their newly-conquered lands into five separate kingdoms between late 7th century and the 9th century. The Arab historian Al-Haqubi in 872 CE mentions Beja kingdoms existing between the Upper Nile and the Red Sea. Each of them had their own sovereign and was independent of the other. Three of them such as Baqlin, Bazin, and Jarin were established within the present day Eritrean territory.

Naqis kingdom extended from Aswan in the north to the lower Barka valley in the south. Its capital city was Hajar. This kingdom comprised of different tribes such as Hadareb, Hijab, Kawbar, Mensa, Rasifa, Arbarba, and Zanfij. The kingdom was strong in its commerce. Hajar was an important center of commerce. The inhabitants of this kingdom were active in the exploitation of gold and other precious stones. In 978 CE, Ibs Hawqal mentioned that the Hadareb tribe claimed to be Muslim though in name only.

Baqlin's territory lay within the present day Eritrean territory. The kingdom encompassed the region of Eritrean plateau, the Sahel, and parts of the Barka valley. Its economic activities were mainly based on agriculture and pastoralism because of controlling considerable rain-fed area. This kingdom had built several cities. Initially, they believed in Az-zabjir as God and Saha Haraga as evil. But gradually, they became Muslim. According to Hawqal, Baqlin had a Muslim king.

Bazin kingdom was situated in Gash and Setit region[2] or we can say between the Atbara and the Barka. Its territory covered the area between the Christian kingdom of Alwa[3] in Nubia and the region of Baqlin. They were at war with Baqlin previously. This kingdom is identified with the present Nara and Kunama people. (Kotler 1966). They were dependent on farming activities. As far as its administrative system is concerned, 'the council of elders' ruled the kingdom.

Like Baqlin and Bazin, the Kingdom of Jarin also encompassed some Eritrean territory. Its domain extended from the coastal town of Massawa[4] in east to Barka in the west and up to Zeila in the south (Somalia). It also included Semhar, Danakil, the Keren and Agordat districts as well as Hall-ad-Dujay. This was a powerful kingdom with a strong king in it's hey day. Bazin had several cities. One of them was the island of Dahlak.

Qata was the southern most of the Beja kingdoms. It was probably situated on the northern border of Hamasien and Seraye between the borders of Badi and a place called Fayakum or Faicun. The people of this kingdom were well known for their braveness and dedication. Qata had a military training school called *Dar as-sawa* that was used to train the young men in arms. Al-Yaqubi in 872 had reported that the Qata kingdom was a tributary to the Abyssinian king. They were also described as Christian and subject to the Aksumite king.

Generally speaking, the main economic activities of these Beja kingdoms consisted of agriculture, cattle herding, mining, and trading. Some of them also lived mainly on hunting and gathering and others forms of nomadic life. They are said to have established 'half nomadic kingdoms.' (Longrigg 1945). In fact, during the four centuries of its rule, the Beja's fuzzy wuzzies pastorals roamed independently throughout the territory of present Eritrea. (ELF). Some of them who penetrated into the Eritrean plateau and northern highlands were converted to settled agriculturists. The tunnels of Medri Zien and the quarry of Meraguz amply corroborate the mining activities of Bejas.

There are numerous vivid local traditions about the Beja domination. The Begattay of the Bilen traditions, the Dina fana of Hamassien customs, and kelew in the highland traditions etc., are the real testimonies of Bejas and in vogue in the Sahel and surroundings regions. Many names of the Beja's places in the central highlands indicate the development of mixed Beja-Habesha culture between 9th and 13th centuries. (Killion 1998). In northern highlands, the Bejas dominated Tigre-speaking tribes. The Beja language belongs to the Northern Cushitic branch of the Afro-Asiatic language family. Over the centuries, Beja language got divided into number of regional dialects, or sub-languages, of which Hedareb is currently spoken in Eritrea.

Most of the Beja remained pagan until the 10th century. However, in the next few centuries number of them got Islamized. They fell under Islamic influence because of the settlement of Muslim traders along the coast and Arab mine-owners and workers in the interior. Massawa and the few ports on the Red Sea became Islamic at an early time. In fact, after the destruction of Adulis, an Islamic culture flourished on the Dahlak Island at the beginning of the 8th century. (Jeslow).

While the peoples of the Eritrean highland districts of Hamasien, Seraye, and Akkele Guzai remained Coptic Christian, Semitic-speaking, agriculturist, and more or less under Abyssinian authority; the peoples of the lowlands and western coastal plains became different in culture and politics. Latter were mainly Muslim, nomadic and pastoralist, and more or less independent of Abyssinian authority. They also had their own government for a time being. But, it is interesting to note that many traditional Beja religious beliefs and practices were retained and a significant degree of syncretism remained among the Beni Amer and other original Beja groups to this day.

At the end of 10th century, a pagan tribe led by a princess known variously as Guedit or Eve invaded the northern Ethiopian highlands with the aim of destroying Christianity and Aksumite imperial power. This was a fatal blow to the reconstructed Abyssinian kingdom. In the 11th century, only the shadow of former Abyssinian power remained. Probably, it lost its hold upon northern regions and the coast. It seems that Islam made in-roads along the Eritrean coast and in the western lowlands. Guedit's massacres of Christians reached into Eritrea and drove many people to seek protection. But, the Bejas continued to hold sway over the Eritrean lowlands. The next Ethiopian kingdom to rise was Zagwe kingdom. It was located in the ancient Agau province of Lasta,[5] the highland region of present day Wollo. Probably, the greatest Zagwe king Lalibela led some expeditions against Islamic forces in the east and along the coast.[6] Its capital city Lalibela[7] or Roha was a walled city. (Greenfield 1980).

Nonetheless, the Beja's dominance over the Eritrean highland was weakened with the migration of Agaw tribes from the Lasta region. This migration began with the rebellion of Gudit in the 10th century and then in the 13th century, when the Solomonic dynasty overthrew the Zagwe dynasty in 1270 CE. During this time, the Belin tribes imposed their hegemony over parts of Eritrean plateau that were formerly controlled by the Bejas. After the 16th century, the Beni Amer confederacy of the western lowlands incorporated most of the Beja-speaking groups in present-day Eritrea. In fact, at present only the Hedareb ethnic group retains its To-Bedawe tongue, although a lot of Beni Amer is bi-lingual (Beja and Tigre and also Arabic).

POPULATION MOVEMENT

The "Post-Aksumite Period" witnessed unprecedented population movements in the present day territory of Eritrea. There were three major groups of people involved in this great migration process such as the highland people of indigenous descent, the Saho, and immigrants of Agew stock. As far as the former is concerned; the Macada, the Gola, the Entertay, and the Loggo constituted the major groups. The Deqqi-minab claimed to have migrated from Dembia-Begemeder. They gave origin to the Deqqi Teshim or Atoshim.[8] The Meretta Keyih and Meretta Sebene resided in the vicinity of Mereb and other streams. The descendants of Akkele and Guzai occupied the Akkele-Guzai region up to Keskese. The Shimazana gave their name to the present Shimezana area.

The Saho began to expand soon after the downfall of Aksum. Their original home was the area south of the Arafali Bay. They spread through various westward areas of Eritrea into the highlands. The Irob set out from northern Dankail through the Laasghide valley. First of all, they reached into eastern Agame and then moved and settled near Meserreha. Irob settled near the Muna River, where Cafna became their center. Subsequent movements brought other Irob groups to the north of the Belesa River in Engela Hatsin and Engela Hames. But, they were again forced out from there and so moved to the Mereb area with the name of Robra. These Irobs also expanded towards Seraye.

Debri Mela is second small Saho division. They settled near Emba-Debri. Today the core group is found in Womberta. The other Saho divisions were the Haso, Tor'a, and Assaworta. These groups moved from the torrid Samotte plains. They went into different directions. The Haso remained in the lower areas. The Tor'a expanded into Semhar. Some of the Tor'a groups continued their movement northwards until they reached the Laba and Anseba rivers. They occupied these areas and made themselves aristocratic rulers of the Mensa and Marya. The Assawarta occupied the region between Akkele-Guzai and the western bank of the Gulf of Arafali.

Another important immigrant group is of Agew Stock. The Agew migrated into Eritrea in two waves. The first migration was around the 10th century CE. These were Bilen of the house of Ghebre Targe. They migrated from Lasta when their land was invaded by a queen from the south.[9] They settled in the Bogos Areas.[10] The next wave of Agew migration was after the downfall of the Zagwe Dynasty in 1270 CE. The Solomonic dynasty came in power blasting the Agew dynasty and began persecuting and killing the Negede Agew for representing the Agew ruling dynasty.

Henceforth, they moved through the Agam territories into Addi Arbate, Digsa, Seraye (Meraguz), Hamassien (Liban), and other smaller villages. They migrated to escape the Amhara onslaught and severe persecution. In the same way, the Adkeme Melga gradually occupied much of the Seraye. After a bitter struggle with the original settlers, the Belew; Atkeme Melga defeated and forced them out to other places. The displaced and surviving Belew groups settled in places such as Tedrer, Deqqi, and Itayes etc. Only the Bilen was able to preserve their language and culture. Nevertheless, other Agew in origin who lived in different parts of Eritrea fused with the local people.[11]

ISLAMIC EXPANSION

The expansion of Islam is an important event in the history of Eritrea during the "Post-Aksumite Period." There are more than 200 Arab inscriptions and historical remains which constitute concrete proof of Islamic expansion in this phase. However, its influence up to the 10th century CE was minimal and limited to the Dahlak Islands, coastal settlements of the Red Sea, and the Gulf of Aden. After the rise of Fatimid in Egypt and the revival of the Red Sea trade, the influence of Islam increased all over the Eritrean region. Islam penetrated into Eritrea and beyond through trade and trade routes. The Dahlak islands were the major gateway to the spread of Islam into Eritrea. It was annexed to the Arab world during the Umayyad rule. In the 10th century, the archipelago fell under the Ziadids of Yemen. However, in the 13th century, Dahlak established its own autonomous Sultanate.[12] Islam was propagated to the nomadic peoples of the coastal lands by the Muslims of Arab origin. Most of these nomads accepted the teaching of Islam and converted in due process.

Thus at last, we can say that the "Post-Aksumite" Eritrean history was dominated by there important phenomenon such as the rule of great Bejas, unprecedented population migration, and the expansion of Islam. The Beja people played an important role in the history of the Eritrean region during the late Aksumite period, when they conquered much of the area and created a new cultural fusion that in some ways set the region apart from the lands south of Mareb River. They were able to control the northern, central, and western parts of the country. An offshoot of Beja's known as the Bellou kingdom, flourished from the 13th to the 16th century in parts of western Eritrea and eastern Sudan. (Connell 2002).

Bejas were able to exploit the resources of this region and achieve a level of prosperity. It was able to combine the agriculture, pastoralism, mining, and trade. Bejas also combined the sedentary as well as nomadic life. They are known for building several cities. Bejas were successful in incorporating the pre-existing inhabitants of the area within its sovereignty. They apparently formed ruling strata over the existing population. (Killion 1998). In fact, it was also an important stage in the history of state formation in this region. Initially, they were pagan with exception of the southern most inhabitants, who accepted Christianity in 500 BCE. Gradually, they were influenced by Islam.

As already mentioned, the other two important landmark of the period under review were the massive population movement and Islamic expansion. Three major groups of people involved in this unprecedented migration process were the highland people of indigenous origin, the Saho, and immigrants of Agew stock. Islam also spread rapidly in the region. It started from the Red Sea coastal region in 8th-9th centuries and penetrated deep into the present day Eritrean territory by 13th-14th centuries.

ENDNOTES

1. Bejas are believed to be close kin of Egyptians.
2. Today it is better known as Gash-Barka zone.
3. Around the beginning of 16th century, a non-Arab power known as Funj sultanate replaced the declining Upper Nubian Christian kingdom of Alwa.
4. Massawa was known as Badi in ancient times.
5. It's in the northern part of present day Ethiopia.

6. But, there is lack of any substantial evidence to corroborate this. It is based on legend.
7. This capital city was named after one of its famous king.
8. It consisted of Minabe Zeray, Tekkele Ageba, and Deqqi Teshim.
9. Probably this queen of south refers to queen Gudit.
10. It is located in the outskirts of Keren.
11. That is why many of the Eritrean of Agew origin are today considered to be Semitic.
12. It was the period of contention in the Arab world.

12

Heritage Management

Eritrea is located on an ancient and intriguing topography. It is also strategically situated as being near to three continents such as Africa, Asia, and Europe. It is blessed with a deep and complex human history. Eritrea possesses several ancient mysteries. It is endowed with immensely diverse archaeological and historical resources; and a very rich flora and fauna. So, it has a huge tourism potential. But, these invaluable resources are under the continuous threat of degradation and destruction due to rapid development, urbanization, industrialization, traditional land distribution, massive infrastructure, development, stone quarrying, and looting and plundering.

HERITAGE POTENTIAL

Undoubtedly, the dependence between history, archaeology, and tourism is very apparent throughout the world. Eritrean history and archaeology has immense potential to develop and contribute to tourism industry in this one of the newest Africa nations. The Eritrean history and archaeology are diverse in time, space, and types. It could provide the tourists the opportunity to understand the human history from earliest to modern times. Such diversity coupled with the breathtaking landscape, crystal clear water of Red Sea, and the long beach line could only prove to be a heaven for the visitors.

HERITAGE GOVERNANCE AND CHALLENGES

The enormous possibilities of Eritrea to throw significant light on human evolution have been limited by disputes of intellectual territory and "research concessions." (Schmidt and Curtis 2008). Present developmental activities are being implemented without a heritage impact assessment. This is evident from the following argument.

> "Large tracts of land are being plotted for construction developments and ways are being bulldozed often without due regard being [sic] had to important cultural heritage sites." (Schmidt 2002a).

There is a national development plan[1] to construct houses, public buildings, and other necessary infrastructures. This threatens historical, archaeological, and cultural heritage badly. One of the big problems is that the areas slated for development are located on the marginal land on which ancient settlements are situated. It is more frustrating because these developments related decisions are irreversible once made. Moreover, the political leaders are puzzled over choosing between two alternatives such as protection of their irreplaceable cultural heritage and the pre-independence promise of land distribution and development. Generally, the latter is expected to take precedence over the former.

This affects the protection and preservation of valuable heritage resources as well as hampers the archaeological and historical researches.[2] There is no comprehensive cultural heritage policy in Eritrea, although it is a party and signatory to the World Heritage Convention (WHC[3]). Eritrea needs to domesticate the international law in order to have effect. It is necessary to bring appropriate implementing legislation to give teeth to regulation of WHC. The present state of heritage policy and subsidiary regulatory tools is certainly not sufficient in that regard. One can say that there is almost a regulatory void in case of cultural heritage protection.[4] A comprehensive policy framework and promulgation of heritage legislation is immediately required. (Habtezion 2008).

This situation becomes further worse in the light of little awareness about heritage-sensitive provisions[5] in existing laws.[6] There is urgent need for the use of such laws. There is some heritage sensitive provisions in existing law especially incase of petroleum and mineral legislation. But, these laws are far from adequate. The matter of monitoring, transparency, penalties, and sanctions are lacking. Another area of major concern is the disfigurement of privately owned cultural heritage such as buildings with historical and architectural values. The disfigurement process of several cultural heritages[7] is widely evident. Moreover like other parts of Africa, the trade in cultural heritage properties is also rampant. (Gebremedhin 1995). It is difficult to prevent such activities in the absence of a substantial prohibiting law. Surprisingly since 2004, a ban has been placed on all foreign funded research projects.

HERITAGE MANAGEMENT

The government could focus on several aspects in order to manage cultural heritage resources. Some of these elements are public education, site conservation, and research. Former should be aimed at all the stakeholders such as government officials, teachers, students, local community, and tourists. Site conservation and management should be supported by appropriate law, public education, and the physical protection. The extensive archaeological exploration and selective excavation needs to be conducted in areas with immediate inevitable development needs. Moreover, an environmental assessment policy guidelines which requires assessment of heritage resources before any developmental activities need to be in place.

Such heritage related developmental, management, and research plan should be inclusive of the needs and sensibilities of local communities. It must ensure their participation into the protection and management of heritage resources. Local communities should also be allowed to derive certain benefits such as employment in the form of site guards, tour guides, and managers out of it. Moreover, representative community management committees that could supervise and interpret a heritage site need to be organized across the country.

Furthermore, a suitable environment and infrastructure is needed for the research.[8] Government has to play a leading role in encouraging and promoting sound academic research. It can also adopt low-budget dissemination techniques of research results through small pamphlets and brochures besides the books. This can also be achieved through proper coordination between academics, concerned government institutions, and public at large. In fact, even the media can be used effectively as a means of mass dissemination of information. The on-site museum[9] is also a viable means through which public education can be achieved.

The active and proper coordination and cooperation among different governmental institutions[10] and NGOs[11] are the need of the day. There should be a national inventory of heritage resources. It should be mandatory for all the developmental activities to fit into this inventory. The recruitment of permanent heritage management officers in concerned ministries[12] for effective and efficient coordination is advisable. For those development projects, which draw foreign funding, each ministry should take the initiative to ensure that the heritage inventories, mitigations, and conservation are adequately financed from those developmental budgets.

SITE MANAGEMENT

Eritrea still lacks an official database of its cultural heritage resources. Perhaps, the heritage sites have not even been comprehensively documented. Moreover, even the available data is not easily accessible.[13] Today, cultural tourism has emerged as an important source of economic benefit to the nation, local community as well as to the heritage sites itself. So, its development has become one of the objectives of heritage institutions and tourist operator throughout the world. (Al Sayyad 2001). One needs to be very careful at the level of operating policies, practices, customer service, partnership, and packaging opportunities. There is need to bring the potential cultural and tourism partners together. One also needs to create tourism partners.[14] It will better understanding between the cultural managers and tourism operator.[15]

The involvement of local community is highly desirable.[16] Any effective archaeological and heritage management must recognize, understand, and address local situations including the needs of local populations. The local community must be involved in the development and management of heritage sites in order to create the contextual framework and enable academic discourse for the interpretation of cultural heritage. They should be imparted the knowledge and importance of their history. The local communities and the academic institutions should be allowed to utilize the heritage resources. (Teka 2002). In fact, the role and actions of local officials are immensely vital in the preservation, protection, and promotion of heritage resources. The heritage management should be based on socio-cultural and socio-environmental setting. Heritage tourism could be sustained only if it meet the needs of the tourists as well as preserve such opportunity for the posterity.

There should be a national heritage management plan consisting of several regional ground plans for sites. Each of them should involve site specific management scheme. It must address certain important issues such as the integration of local community in direct day-to-day site management, conservation of site for further development, academic research, utilization of income for the sustainability of the resources as well as the local community. There should be a plan for the investigation and study of social and cultural organization around the site, conservation programs, landscape study[17] and human development.[18] There is requirement of the development of a social assessment which should include study of the social and political structure of the local community and geo-ecological setting of the area; identification and assessment of the potential socio-economic benefits from the contiguous heritage sites; study of current land-use management and economic activities; and development of a new land use management plan if necessary. One should also facilitate the formation of a local management committee. Thereafter, it is necessary to work with the latter. The participation of local management committees in the design and planning process; and in the implementation and monitoring of the plan; and representation of their views and concerns should be ensured.

One of the pertinent issues is the institutional response to heritage resources. There is immediate need of reformation and restructuring of the concerned institutions. The skilled manpower in archaeology[19] requires to be better utilized. They should be utilized in documentation, preservation, and management of heritage sites. The concerned institution needs to organize a systematic public awareness program to popularize and conserve the nation's irreplaceable heritage resources. It is necessary to involve all the stakeholders[20] in such kind of program. A mutually beneficial partnership needs to be developed between all the stakeholders. On the one hand, all tourism plans must take care of heritage related issue from the very beginning stage; where as on the other hand, all heritage management plans must address the need and perspective of tourism industry. First of all, there is need of careful investigation and documentation of archaeological sites. It should be followed by erection of tourism and associated recreational facilities. Then a responsible marketing of tourism and heritage is desired. It must be consistent with the significance of the concerned place.[21]

Eritrea has all the potential to become a center of archaeo-tourism. It could earn huge income from this. This income could be further utilized for the study, preservation, protection and promotion[22] of numerous heritage resources throughout the length and breadth of the country. There is also need of clear cut standards and guidelines to develop, maintain, and sustain appropriate heritage plans, policies, and facilities. That should have enough space for the local communities, good research, and public awareness and support. The problem is compounded by lack of comprehensive legal framework aimed at cultural heritage.

The government needs to develop a comprehensive policy on cultural heritage and back it with necessary legal tools for more effectiveness. However, till that happen one can also strive to use the cultural heritage related provisions in the existing legal system. Moreover, there is urgent need of partnership between all the stakeholders. That should be followed by comprehensive management and development plan in which heritage resources could enhance tourism that sustains the concerned resources as well as the local populace.

ENDNOTES

1. It has come into existence since 2002.
2. National Museum is practically having its final say in the acceptance, evaluation, permission or rejection of any research proposal. Sometimes, these proposals become victim of poor communication, bureaucratic red-tapism, unnecessary delay, and power-politics between institutions.
3. World Heritage Convention was held in 1972. It is one of the international regulatory tools that seek to preserve the world's "most outstanding" natural and cultural heritage site. WHC also seeks to enhance and encourage international cooperation in this regard. It underlines the duty of member states to ensure legal and administrative tools to identify, protect, conserve, present, and rehabilitate their heritage.
4. It is more appalling in the light of continuous destruction of material culture.
5. Article 21/4 of the Constitution of Eritrea affirms the responsibility of the state to preserve its cultural heritage. It says "The State and society shall have the responsibility of identifying, preserving and developing...historical and cultural heritage." So, the state is constitutionally mandated to provide a favourable environment for the promotion of cultural heritage. It also sets the necessary foundation for future development of a cultural heritage policy. Article 17 of the Petroleum Proclamation No. 40/1993 says that a contractor shall "conduct petroleum operations in a manner designed to protect anthropological, archaeological and historical objects and, sites...notify the minister...not to remove from their locations, any anthropological,

archaeological and historical objects...without the prior written authorization of the minister." Article 6 of Proclamation No. 68/1995 provides that the government can exclude any area from mining operations, particularly in regard to sites of historical, cultural, or religious interests...Article 13 (Excluded Areas) of Legal Notice No. 19/1995 provides that "Unless the licensing authority decides otherwise, no license shall be issued for any area which is with in 100 meters of a site of archaeological, cultural, or religious importance..." The trade in cultural heritage properties is punishable as (Government of Eritrea, Art. 642/2, Transitional Penal Code of Eritrea, 1957) the existing law says that "misappropriation or abstraction...of historical archaeological or artistic objects...is punishable under the ordinary provision regarding theft, breach of trust to the nature of the offence." Moreover, Article 803 of the code says that "a person is punishable...if he/she contravenes the rules and regulation of protecting the national, historical, archaeological and artistic wealth." It further regulates that any person who impairs the value of, defaces or puts in jeopardy any historical or archaeological monument is also punishable.

6. It is very evident by the rare invocation of such laws on behalf of cultural heritage.
7. One of the examples is colonial buildings.
8. Documentation and digitalization of data is needed to support future archaeological research. It should also be supported by a favourable environment which respects the diverse opinion on history.
9. It is especially possible on the large and very important sites. Moreover, it should be done in a way that is sustainable and managed through the local community and decentralized control.
10. It requires appropriate communication between National Museum, other responsible institution, and several ministries in placement of archaeology and anthropology graduates and interns.
11. It refers to Non Governmental Organizations.
12. It refers to those ministries and institution, which are responsible for heritage resources.
13. The National Museum of Eritrea does document the heritage sites on impromptu basis. But even these data are not available to researchers and agencies very easily.

14. The potential tourism partners could be Ministry of Tourism, National Museum of Eritrea, and Travel Agencies.
15. It would help them to understand the needs of each other. This would lead to development of mutually beneficial programs.
16. First of all, the heritage belongs to them. Secondly, the access to cultural property would restore their damaged self-confidence and also develop a sense of ownership and pride. All these would help them to see the need for the survival of their heritage locales.
17. It should include the study physical and environmental aspect of the site.
18. Human development may involve the study of community impact, creating the public awareness, imparting education, and promoting tourism.
19. Dozens of young archaeology graduates has been produced from University of Asmara and College of Arts and Social Sciences. Presently, they have been deputed as interns and graduate assistants in National Museum of Eritrea, Ministry of Tourism and Institute of Higher Learning such as College of Arts and Social Sciences.
20. The stakeholders include local population, academic community, students, government officials, NGOs, and religious leaders.
21. Otherwise, it would lead to tourist estrangement and disillusionment.
22. The promotion activity might include marketing of heritage sites; and building of recreational facilities, historic parks, and on-site museums.

Bibliography

Abbate, E., et al. 1998. A one-million-year-old Homo cranium from the Danakil (Afar) Depression of Eritrea. *Nature* 393: 458-460.

– – – 2004. Geology of the Homo-bearing Pleistocene Dandiero Basin (Buia region, Eritrean Danakil Depression). *Rivisita Italiana di paleontologia e stratigrafia* 110, Supplement: 5-34.

Abir, Mordechai. 1980. *Ethiopia and the Red Sea: The rise and decline of the Solomonic dynasty and Moslem-European rivalry in the region.* Jerusalem.

Al Sayyad, N. 2001. Global norms and urban forms in the age of tourism: Manufacturing heritage, consuming tradition. In *Consuming tradition, manufacturing heritage, global norms and urban forms in the age of tourism.* ed. N. Al Sayyad. 1-33. London: Rutledge.

Alam, Hudud al. 1937. *The regions of the world, A Persian geographer, 982 AD.* trans. V. Minorsky. Oxford: University Press.

Ambrose, S. H. 2003. Population bottleneck. In *Genetics.* ed. R. Robinson. 167-171.

Anfray, F. 1965. Chronique Archeologique (1960-64). *Annales d'Ethiopie* 6:3-48.

– – – 1966. Laooterie de Matara. *Rassegna di studi Etiopici* 22: 5-74.

– – – 1967. Matara. *Annales d'Ethiopie* 7:33-88.

– – – 1968. Aspects de l'archeologie ethiopienne. *Journal of African History* 9:345-366.

– – – 1970. Notes archeologiques. *Annales d'Ethiopie* 8:31-42.

– – – 1974. Deux villes Axoumites: Adoulis et Matara. *Atti IV congresso internationale di studi Etiopici.* Rome. 745-765.

– – – 1981. The civilization of Aksum from the first to the seventh century. In *General History of Africa II, Ancient civilizations of Africa*, ed. G. Mokhtar. 362-379. Paris: UNESCO.

– – – 1994. *Eritrea: Preservation and presentation of the cultural heritage.* Restricted Technical Report. Paris: UNESCO.

Anfray, F., and G. Annequin. 1965. Matara: Deuxieme, troisieme et quatrieme campagnes de fouilles. *Annales d'Ethiopie* 6: 49-92.

Anon. 1988. *Historical truth about Eritrea.*

Arkell, A. J. 1954. Four occupation sites at Agrodat. *Kush* 2.

Bairu, Tafla. 1994. Interdependence through independence: The challenges of Eritrean historiography. *New trends in Ethiopian studies* 1.

Bard, K. A., M. Coltorti, M. Di Blasi, F. Dramis, and R. Fattovich. 2000. The environmental History of Tigray (Northern Ethiopia) in the middle and late Holocene: A preliminary outline. *African archaeological review* 17(2): 65-86.

Bar-Yosef, O., and A. Belfer-Cohen. 2001. From Africa to Eurasia- Early dispersals. *Quaternary International* 75: 19-28.

Bent, J. T. 1896. *The sacred city of the Ethiopians being a record of travel and research in Abyssinia in 1893.* London: Longmans, Green and Co.

– – – 1893. The ancient trade route across Ethiopia. *Geo. Journal* 2.

Beyin, Amanuel, and John Shea. 2008. Evidence for middle and later stone age cultures on the Buri Peninsula and Gulf of Zula, Red Sea coast of Eritrea. In *The Archaeology of ancient Eritrea.* ed. Peter R. Schmidt, Matthew C. Curtis and Zelalem Teka. Trenton and Asmara: The Red Sea Press, Inc.

Blue, Lucy, Yohannes Gebreyesus, Darren Glazier, Daniel Habtemichael, David Peacock, and Rezene Russom. 2008. Assessing ancient Adulis: Recent investigations of the ancient Red Sea port. In *The Archaeology of Ancient Eritrea.* ed. Peter R. Schmidt, Matthew C. Curtis, and Zelalem Teka. Trenton and Asmara: The Red Sea Press, Inc.

Blundell, Weld. 1922. *The royal chronicle of Abyssinia.* Rome.

Boardman, S. 1999. The agricultural foundation of the Aksumite Empire, Ethiopia: An interim report. In *The exploitation of plant resources in ancient Africa.* ed. M. Van Der Veen. 137-148. New York: Kluwer Academic Publishers.

– – – 2000. Archaeobotany. In *Archaeology at Aksum, Ethiopia, 1993-7.* Vols. 1 and 2. ed. D. W. Phillipson, 363-368, 412-414, 468-470. London: The British Institute in Eastern Africa and the Society of Antiquaries.

Brandt, S.A., and N. Carder. 1987. Pastoral rock art in the Horn of Africa: Making sense of udder chaos. *World Archaeology* 19(2): 194-213.

– – – 1986. The upper Pleistocene and early Holocene Prehistory of the Horn of Africa. *African Archaeological Review* 4: 41-82.

Bruggemann, H. J., et al. 2004. Stratigraphy, palaeoenvironments and model for the deposition of the Abdur Reef limestone: Context for an important archaeological site from the last interglacial on the Red Sea coast of Eritrea. *Palaeogeography, palaeoclimatology, palaeoecology,* 203: 179-206.

Budge, E. A. T. Wallis. 1928. *History of Ethiopia, Nubia & Abyssinia* (according to the hieroglyphic inscriptions of Egypt and Nubia, and the Ethiopian chronicles), Vol. 1. London: Methuen & Co.

– – – 1928. *The book of saints of the Ethiopian church.* Cambridge: Cambridge University Press.

– – – 1966. *A History of Ethiopia.* Netherlands: Cosferhout N. B. Vol. 1.

Butzer, K. 1981. Rise and fall of Axum: A geoarchaeological interpretation. *American Antiquity* 46: 471-495.

Buxton, D. R. 1947. Christian antiquities of northern Ethiopia. *Archaeologia* 92: 1-42.

Buxton, D. R., and D. Matthews. 1974. The reconstruction of vanished Aksumite buildings. *Rassegna di studi Etiopici* 25: 53-76.

Cain, R. C. 2000. Archaezoology. In *Archaeology at Aksum, Ethiopia, 1993-7.* Vols. 1 and 2. ed. D. W. Phillipson, 218, 369-372, 414-417, 510-511. London: The British Institute in Eastern Africa and the Society of Antiquaries.

Calegari, G. I. 1999. Repertorio ragionato ed esegesi iconografica (Memorie della societa Italiana di scienze naturali e del museo civico di storia naturale di Milano). In *L'arte upestre dell'Eritrea.* Milan: Societa Italiana di Scienze Naturalie e del Museo Civico di Storia Naturale di Milano.

Casson, L. 1989. *The Periplus maris Erythraei.* Princeton, NJ: Princeton University Press.

Cerulli, E. 1988. Ethiopia's relations with the Muslim world. *General History of Africa - Africa from Seventh to Eleventh Centuries*, Vol. 3. Berkeley: UNESCO.

Cervicek, P. 1976. Rock engravings from the Hamasen region, Eritrea. *Paideuma* 22: 237-256.

Chittick, N. 1974. Excavations at Aksum 1973-74. A preliminary report. *Azania* 9: 159-205.

– – – Radiocarbon dates from Aksum. *Azania* 11: 179-181.

Connah, Graham. *African Civilizations - An Archaeological Perspective.* Cambridge University Press.

Connell, Dan. ed. 2002. *Eritrea - A country handbook.* Asmara.

Contenson, Henri de. 1981. Pre-Aksumite Culture. In *General History of Africa - Ancient civilizations of Africa.* ed. G. Mokhtar. Vol. 2. Berkeley: UNESCO.

Crowfoot, J. W. 1911. Some Red Sea ports in the Anglo-Egyptian Sudan. *Geo. J.* 27 (5).

Curtis, M. C. 2004. Ancient interaction across the southern Red Sea: New suggestions for cultural exchange and complex societies during the first millennium BC. In *Trade and travel in the Red Sea region.* eds. P. Lunde and A. Porter. 57-70. Oxford: Archaeopress.

– – – 2005 "Archaeological investigations in the Greater Asmara area: A regional approach in the central highlands of Eritrea". PhD dissertation. University of Florida.

Curtis, M. C., and Daniel Habtemichael. 2008. Matara, Keskese, and the classical period archaeology of the Akele Guzay highlands: A brief overview. In *The archaeology of ancient Eritrea.* eds. Peter R. Schmidt, Matthew C. Curtis, and Zelalem Teka ed. Trenton and Asmara: The Red Sea Press, Inc.

Curtis, M. C., and Peter R. Schmidt. 2008. Landscape, people, and places on the ancient Asmara plateau. In *The archaeology of ancient Eritrea.* eds. Peter R. Schmidt, Matthew C. Curtis, and Zelalem Teka ed. Trenton and Asmara: The Red Sea Press, Inc.

D'Andrea, A. C., and M. Haile. 2002. Traditional emmer processing in highland Ethiopia. *Journal of Ethnobiology* 22 (2): 179-217.

D'Andrea, A. C., D. Lyons, M. Haile, and A. Butler. 1999. Ethnoarchaeological approaches to the study of prehistoric agriculture in the highlands of Ethiopia. In *The exploitation of plant resources in ancient Africa.* ed. M. Van Der Veen. 101-122. New York: Kluwer Academic/Plenum Publishers.

D'Andrea, A. C., Peter R. Schmidt, and Matthew C. Curtis. 2008. Paleoethnobotanical analysis and agricultural economy at early 1st millennium BCE sites around Asmara. In *The archaeology of ancient Eritrea.* eds. Peter R. Schmidt, Matthew C. Curtis, and Zelalem Teka ed. Trenton and Asmara: The Red Sea Press, Inc.

Dehenseler, Max. *An Atlas of Ethiopia.*

Denison, Edward, and Edward Paice. eds. 2002. *Eritrea- The Bradt travel guide.* England.

Desanges, J. 1969. D'Axoum a I'Assam, aux portes de la Chine; le voyage du scholastcus de Thebes (Entre 360 et 500 aptes J-C). *Historia* 18:5.

Doresse, Jean. 1959. *Ancient cities and temples- Ethiopia.* trans. Elsa Coult. London: Elerk Books Ltd.

Drewes, A. J. 1954. The inscription from Dibdib in Erythrea. *Bibliotheca Orientalis* 11: 185-186.

– – – 1956. Nouvelles inscriptions de I'Ethiopie. *Bibliotheca orientalis* 13: 179-182.

– – – 1962 *Inscriptions de I'Ethiopie antique.* Leiden, the Netherlands: E. J. Brill.

Duncanson, D. J. 1947. Girmaten: A new archeological site in Eritrea. *Antiquity* 27.

– – – 1952. Eritrean rock sculptures. *Man* 52.

Ehret, C. F. 1979. On the antiquity of agriculture in Ethiopia. *JAH* 20.

Eigner, D. 1998. Preliminary report on season 1997. G.A.M.E. Manuscript.

– – – 1999. German archaeological mission to Eritrea, season 1996. The ruin "Littmann no. 8" at Qohaito. *Mare Erythraeum* 3: 41-56.

ELF. *Eritrea: History-Geography-Economy*

– – – *Eritrean ethnic groups.*

– – – *Eritrean history: Collections of the different tribe/nations.*

– – – *The History of Eritrea.*

Fattovich, R. 1977. Pre-Aksumite civilization of Ethiopia: A preliminary review. *Proceedings of the seminar fro Arabian studies* Vol. 7.

– – – 1980. Materiali per lo studio della ceramica pre-Aksumita Etiopica. *Annali della istitutio orientale di Napoli* 25. Napoli: Instituto Orientale di Napoli.

– – – 1984. Data for the History of the ancient peopling of the northern Ethiopia- Sudanese borderland. In *Proc. Seventh ICES.* ed. S. Rubenson. Addis Ababa.

– – – 1988. Remarks on the late pre-history and early history of northern Ethiopia. *Proc. Eighth ICES.* Vol. 1. Addis Ababa.

– – – 1990. Remarks on the pre-Aksumite period in northern Ethiopia. *Journal of Ethiopian Studies* 23: 1-33.

– – – 1993. The gash group of the eastern Sudan: An outline. In *Environmental change and human culture in the Nile Basin and northern Africa until the second millennium BC.* eds. M. Kobusiewicz, and J. Alexander. 439-448. Poland: Poznan Archaeological Museum.

– – – 2000. *Aksum and the Habashat: State and ethnicity in ancient northern Ethiopia and Eritrea.* Working Papers in African Studies, No. 228. Boston: African Studies Center, Boston University.

Fattovich, R., K. A. Bard, L. Petrassi, and V. Pisano. 2000. *The Aksum archaeological area: A preliminary assessment.* Naples, Italy: Istituto Unversitario Orientale.

Faure, H., R. C. Walter, and D. R. Grant. 2002. The coastal oasis: Ice age springs on emerged continental shelves. *Global and planetary change* 33: 47-56.

Flohn, H., and S. Nicholson. 1980. Climatic fluctuations in the arid belt of the old world since the last glacial maximum. In *Paleoecology of Africa and the surrounding islands.* eds. E. M. van Zinderen Bakker et al. Rotterdam.

Gebrehiwet, Girmay, et al. 2008. The Eritrean national museum- A cultural heritage. Senior Essay. College of Arts and Social Sciences. Mai-Nefi, Eritrea.

Gebremedhin, N. 1995. Introductory remarks. In *National environmental management plan.* Government of Eritrea, Asmara.

Gilkes, P. 1991. Eritrea: Historiography and methodology. *African affairs* 99.

Greenfield, R. *Eritrean History- Pre-colonial and colonial.*

– – – 1980. Pre-colonial and colonial History. In *Behind the war in Eritrea.* eds. Davidson, et al. Nottingham: Spokesman.

Haberland, E. 1992. The Horn of Africa. In *General History of Africa- Africa from the sixteenth to the eighteenth century.* ed. B. A. Ogot. Vol. 5. Berkeley: UNESCO.

Habte Sellassie, Sergew. 1972. *Ancient and medieval Ethiopian history to 1270.* Addis Ababa.

Habtemichael, D. 2002. The "Sabean man's burden," questioning dominant historical paradigms with new archeological findings, and Keskese Valley archaeological survey report. M. A. paper. Department of Anthropology. University of Florida.

– – – 2004 The "Sabean man's burden: Questioning the dominant historical paradigm with new archaeological findings at Keskese Valley. *Journal of Eritrean Studies* 3 (2): 25-52.

Habtezion, Zerisenay D. 2008. Heritage governance in Eritrea: Reality and choices. In *The Archaeology of Ancient Eritrea.* ed. Peter R. Schmidt, Matthew C. Curtis, and Zelalem Teka. Trenton and Asmara: The Red Sea Press, Inc.

Harden, J. M. 1926. *An introduction to Ethiopic Christian literature.* London.

Haughton, G. C. 1830. Account of an ancient Arabic grave-stone found at Dahlac el-Kibeer near Massowah, Abyssinia. *Royal Asiatic society, transactions* 2.

Hourani, G. F. 1951. *Arab seafaring in the Indian Ocean in ancient and early medieval times.* Princeton, NJ: Princeton University Press.

Huntingford, G. W. B. 1980. *The periplus of the Erythraean Sea.* London: Hakluyt Society.

Ibn-Khaldun. 1892. *Yemen, its early medieval History.* trans. H. C. Kay. London.

Irvine, A. K. 1965. On the identity of the Habashat in the south Arabian inscriptions. *ISS* 10.

Iyesus, Abba Isaak Ghebre. 2000. *Ethiopian syndrome.* trans. Amanuel Sahle. Asmara: MBY Publishing and Printing Press.

Jaeger, O. *Antiquities of north Ethiopia.* Stuttgart.

Jamme, A. 1962. *Sabean inscriptions from Mahram Bilqis, Marib.* Baltimore.

Jeslow, Jasman. *The wonders of Eritrea.*

Jewsiewicki, Bogumil, and David Newbury eds. 1986. *African historiographies: What History for which Africa.* London and New Delhi.

Johanson, D., and B. Edgar. 1996. *From Lucy to language.* New York: Simons Schuster Editions.

Jones, A. H. M., and Elizabeth Monroe. 1955. *A History of Ethiopia.* Oxford, London.

Jones, Scott. 1991. Archaeological and environmental observations in Rora Habab, Eritrea. *Azania* 26.

Kahsay, Habtom & Tsegai Medin, Amaha Segid, and Tekleab Haile. 2008, Der'a-Hawatsu archaeological investigation. In *Paleoanthropological and archeo-historical research on Eritrea.* ed. Tekeste Melake. Asmara: National Museum of Eritrea.

Killion, Tom. 1996. The Eritrean economy in historical perspective. *ESR* 1 (1).

– – – 1998. *Historical dictionary of Eritrea.* London.

Kingdon, J. 1993. *Self-made man: Human evolution from Eden to extinction.* New York: John Wiley.

Kirwan, L. P. 1972. The Christian topography and the kingdom of Axum. *The geographical journal* 138 (2): 166-177.

Kobishchanov, Y. M. 1966. The origin of Ethiopian literature. Essays on African Cultures.

– – – 1966. The sea voyages of ancient Ethiopians in the Indian Ocean. *Proc. Third ICES.* Vol. 1. Addis Ababa.

– – – 1979. *Axum.* University Park, Philadelphia: Pennsylvania State University Press.

– – – 1981. Aksum: Political system, economics and culture, first to fourth century. In *General History of Africa II: Ancient civilizations of Africa.* ed. G. Mokhtar. 381-400. Berkeley: University of California Press.

Kotler, Neil G. 1966. *History of Eritrea.* Asmara: HSIU.

Kruger, T., and M. Pospis. 1997. Geodatische arbeiten auf dem plateau von Qohaito wahrend der G.A.M.E. Report submitted to the National Museum of Eritrea by the German Archaeological Mission to Eritrea.

Lefebvre, T. 1845-49. *Voyage en Abyssinie execute pendant les annees 1839-1843.* Vols. 6. Paris: Histoire Naturelle-Zoologie.

Lewis-Williams, J. 1991. Wrestling with analogy: A methodological dilemma in upper Paleolithic art research. *Proceedings of the prehistoric society.* 57 (1) 149-162.

– – – 1986. Cognitive and optical illusions in San rock art research. *Current Anthropology.* 27 (2) 171-177.

Libsekal, Yosief. 2008. The development of ancient complex society and early development system of Qohaito. In *Paleoanthropological and archeo-historical research on Eritrea.* ed. Tekeste Melake. Asmara: National Museum of Eritrea.

Littmann E., D. Krencker, and T. Von Lupke. 1913, *Deutsche Aksum-expedition.* Berlin: Reimer.

Longrigg, Stephen H. 1945. *A short history of Eritrea.* Oxford: Clarendon P.

Macaulay, V., et al. 2005. Single, rapid coastal settlement of Asia revealed by analysis of complete mitochondrial genomes. *Science* 308: 103-1036.

Mathew, G. 1976. The dating and significance of the *periplus of the Erythrean Sea.* In *East Africa and the orient.* ed. H. N. Chittick, and R. Rotberg. London.

McBrearty, S., and A. Brooks. 2000. The revolution that wasn't: A new interpretation of the origin of modern human behavior. *Journal of human evolution* 39: 453-563.

McDougall, I., F. H. Brown, and J. G. Fleagle. 2005. Stratigrapic placement and age of modern humans from Kibish. *Nature* 433 (17): 733-736Ethiopia.

Medin, Tsegai. 2008. The discovery of new hominid evidence. In *Paleoanthropological and Archeo-Historical Research on Eritrea.* ed. Tekeste Melake. Asmara: National Museum of Eritrea.

Mekouria, Tekle Tsadik. 1981. Christian Axum. In *General History of Africa-Ancient Civilizations of Africa.* ed. G. Mokhtar. Vol. 2. UNESCO. Berkeley.

– – – 1988. The Horn of Africa. In *General History of Africa- Africa from Seventh to Eleventh Centuries.* ed. M. el Fasi. Vol. 3. UNESCO. Berkeley.

Michels, J. W. 1994. Regional political organization in the Axum-Yeha area during the Pre-Aksumite and Aksumite eras. In *Etudes ethiopiennes: actes de la conference internationale des etudes ethiopiannes.* ed. C. Lapage. Vol. 1. 61-80. Paris: Societe Francaise Pour les Etudes Ethiopiennes.

Monneret de Villard, U. 1940. L'inscrizione etiopica di Ham e l'Epigrafia meroitica. *Aegyptus* 20: 61-68.

Mordini, A. 1960. Gli aurei Kushana del convento di Dabra-Dammo. *Atti del Convegno Internazionale di Studi Etiopici* 2-4: 249-254.

Munro-Hay, S. C. 1981-82. A tyranny of sources: The history of Aksum from its coinage. *NEAS* 3 (3).

– – – 1982. The foreign trade of the Aksumite port of Adulis. *Azania* 17: 107-125.

– – – 1984. *The coinage of Aksum.* New Delhi.

– – – 1989a. Aksumite chronology; some reconsiderations. *Proc. Eighth ICES.* Vol. 2. Addis Ababa.

– – – 1989b. British Museum excavations at Adulis, 1868. *Antiquaries ojurnal* 39 (1): 43-52.

– – – ed. 1989c. *Excavations at Aksum: An account of research at the ancient Ethiopian capital directed in 1972-74 by Dr. Neville Chittick.* London: The British Institute in Eastern Africa.

– – – 1990. The rise and fall of Aksum: Chronological considerations. *JES.* 23.

– – – 1991. *Aksum: An African civilisation of late antiquity.* Edinburgh, Scotland: Edinburgh University Press.

– – – 1996. Aksumite overseas interests. In *The Indian Ocean in antiquity.* ed. J. Reade. 403-416. London: Kegan Paul International, in association with the British Museum.

Negash, Agazi. 1997. The rock Art in Ethiopia and the Horn. In Joseph O. Vogel ed. *Encyclopedia of pre-colonial Africa.* Walnut Creek, CA: AltaMira Press.

Negussie, Caroline 1994. Aksum and Matara: A stratigraphic comparison of two Aksumite towns. In *New Trends in Ethiopian Studies.* ed. H. Marcus. Vol. 1. Lawrenceville: Red Sea Press.

Okubay, Werede. 2008. The role of ancient Ona sites in the development of the Eritrean tourism industry: An insider's perspective. In *The Archaeology of Ancient Eritrea.* ed. Peter R. Schmidt, Matthew C. Curtis, and Zelalem Teka. Trenton and Asmara: The Red Sea Press, Inc.

Pankhurst, R. 1961. *An introduction to the economic history of Ethiopia, from early times to 1800.* London.

– – – 1974. The history of Ethiopia's relations with India prior to the nineteenth century. *IV Congresso Internazionale di Studi Ethiopici* 1: 205-311.

– – – 1984. Early Pharaonic contacts with the Land of Punt. *QSE* 5.

Paribeni, R. 1907. Richerche nel luogo dell'antica Adulis. *Monumenti Antichi, Reale Accademia dei Lincei* 18: 438-572.

Peacock, D., D. Williams, and S. James. 2006. Basalt as ships' ballast and the Roman Incense trade. In *Food for the Gods: New light on the ancient incense trade.* eds. D. Peacock, and D. Williams.

Pearson, J. 2002. *Shamanism and the ancient mind: A cognitive approach to archaeology.* Walnut Creek, CA: AltaMira Press.

Petraglia, D. M. 2003. The lower Paleolithic of the Arabian Peninsula: Occupation, adaptation, and dispersal. *Journal of World Prehistory.* 17: 141-179.

Phillipson, D. W. 1997. *The monuments of Aksum.* Addis Ababa: Addis Ababa University.

– – – 1998. *Ancient Ethiopia: Aksum, its antecedents and successors.* London: British Museum Press.

Philliposn D. W., and A. Reynolds. 1996. B. I. E.A. excavations at Aksum, northern Ethiopia, 1995. *Azania.* 31: 99-147.

Phillipson, D. W. ed. 2000. *Archaeology at Aksum, Ethiopia, 1993-7.* London: British Institute in Eastern Africa and the Society of Antiquaries of London.

Pirenne, J. 1987. The chronology of ancient South Arabia- Diversity of opinion. In *Yemen.* ed. Innsbruck.

Plant, R. 1978. A hypothesis on origins of Ethiopian architecture. *Abbay* 9: 21-24.

Plant, Ruth. 1985. *Architecture of the Tigray, Ethiopia.* England: Ravens Educational and Development Services Ltd.

Pliny. 1938-62. *Natural History.* Vols. 11. trans. H. Rackman. Cambridge: Harvard University Press.

Pollero, Alberto. 1996. *The native peoples of Eritrea.* Rome.

Pool, David. *Ethiopia and Eritrea, The pre colonial period.* Manchester University.

Ptolemy, Claudius. 1932. *Geography of Claudius Ptolemy.* trans. E. Stevenson. New York.

Rena, Ravinder. 2007. Historical development of money and banking in Eritrea from the Axumite kingdom to the present. *African and Asian Studies*. New York: Brill for Afro-Asian Association 6 (1&2): 135-153.

Rose, I. J. 2004a. New evidence for the expansion of an upper Pleistocene population out of East Africa, from the site of station one, northern Sudan. *Cambridge archaeological journal* 14 (2): 205-216.

– – – 2004b. The question of upper Pleistocene connections between East Africa and South Arabia. *Current anthropology* 45 (4): 551-555.

Rossini, Carlo Conti. *The history of Ethiopia: Part One.*

– – – *The history of Ethiopia: Part Two*

– – – 1901. L'evangelo d'oro di Dabra Libanos. *Rendiconti della reale academia dei lincei.* 10 (5).

– – – 1990. Ricerche e studi sull'Etiopia. *Bollenttino dell societa geografica Italiana* 4(1): 104-120.

Sabby, Othman Saleh. 1974. *The history of Eritrea.* trans. Muhamad Fawaz al-Azem. Lebanon: Dar Al-Masirah.

Sadr, K. 1991. *The development of nomadism in ancient northeast Africa.* Philadelphia: University of Pennsylvania Press.

Sayce, A. 1909. A Greek inscription of a king (?) of Aksum found at Meroe. *Proceeding of society Biblical archaeology.* 31.

Schmidt, P. R. 2002a. The "Ona" culture of Greater Asmara: Archaeology's liberation of Eritrea's ancient history from colonial paradigms. *Journal of Eritrean Studies* 1:29-58.

– – – 2002b. Saving Asmara's ancient heritage. *University of Asmara College of Arts and Social Sciences Review* 1:11-12.

Schmidt, P. R., and M. C. Curtis. 2001. Urban precursors in the Horn: Early 1st millennium BC communities in Eritrea. *Antiquity* 75 (290): 849-859.

Schmidt, P. R., and M. C. Curtis. 2008. The development of archaeology in Eritrea. In *The Archaeology of ancient Eritrea.* ed. Peter R. Schmidt, Matthew C. Curtis and Zelalem Teka. Trenton and Asmara: The Red Sea Press, Inc.

Schmidt, P. R., C. Naeser, Z. Teka, D. Habtemichael, M. C. Curtis, Y. Mobae, A. G. Mehari, and M. Weldai. 2004. The antiquity of settlement in the southern Eritrean highlands: An Eritro-American-German collaborative project. A research design submitted to the University of Asmara.

Schmidt, P. R., M. C. Curtis, and Zelalem Teka 2008. The ancient ona communities of the first millennium BCE: Urban precursors and independent development on the asmara plateau', In *The Archaeology of ancient Eritrea.* ed. Peter R. Schmidt, Matthew C. Curtis and Zelalem Teka. Trenton and Asmara: The Red Sea Press, Inc.

Selassie, Kiros Habte, and Mazengia Dina. eds. 1969. *Ethiopia- A short illustrated history.* Addis Ababa: Ministry of Education and Fine Arts, Imperial Ethiopian Government.

Semaw, S., et al. 1997. 2.5 million year old stone tools from Gona, Ethiopia. *Nature* 385, 333-336.

Shinnie, P. 1955. The fall of Meroe. *Kush* 3.

– – – 1967. *Meroe.* London.

Shoshani, Jeheskel, Merih W. Ghebregiorgis, and Peter R. Schmidt. 2008. Interpretations of faunal remains from archeological sites on the Asmara plateau of Eritrea. In *The Archaeology of ancient Eritrea.* ed. Peter R. Schmidt, Matthew C. Curtis and Zelalem Teka. Trenton and Asmara: The Red Sea Press, Inc.

Siravo, Francisco. 1997. Establishment of the national museum and renovation of Asmara theatre. Paris.

Soni, Raman Kumar. 2007. *Incredible Egypt: The history of early Egyptian civilization.* Delhi: Radha Publication.

Steven A. Brandt, Andrea Manzo, and Cinzia Perlingieri. 2008. Linking the highlands and lowlands: Implications of a test excavation at Kokan rockshelter, Agordat, Eritrea. In *The Archaeology of ancient Eritrea.* ed. Peter R. Schmidt, Matthew C. Curtis and Zelalem Teka. Trenton and Asmara: The Red Sea Press, Inc.

Strabo 1940. *The geography of Strabo.* Vols. 8. ed. H. L. Jones. London.

Stringer, C. 2002. The morphological and behavioral origins of modern humans. In *The Speciation of Homo Sapiens, Proceedings of the British Academy.* ed. T. J. Crow. 106: 23-30.

Sundstrom, R. 1907. Report on an expedition to Adulis. *Zeitschrift fur Assyriologie* 20:171-182.

Tamrat, Tadesse. 1972. *Church and state in Ethiopia* 1270-1527. Oxford: Clarendon Press.

Tchernov, E. 1992. Biochronology, paleoecology, and dispersal events of hominids in the southern Levant. In *The evolution and dispersal of modern humans in Asia.* eds. T. Akazawa, K. Aoki, and T. Kimura. 149-188. Tokyo: Hokusen-sha.

Tedla, Aradom. 1964. *Facts about Eritrea.* Asmara

Teka, Zelalem. 2002. Rock art sites in the area of Addi Keyih, Eritrea. *Journal of Eritrean Studies* 1: 1-22.

Teka, Zelalem. 2008. Distribution and significance of ancient rock art sites in Eritrea. In *The Archaeology of ancient Eritrea.* ed. Peter R. Schmidt, Matthew C. Curtis and Zelalem Teka. Trenton and Asmara: The Red Sea Press, Inc.

Teka, Zelalem, and Dawit Okubatsion 2008. Lithic artifacts from archaeological sites in the Greater Asmara Area. In *The Archaeology of ancient Eritrea.* ed. Peter R. Schmidt, Matthew C. Curtis and Zelalem Teka. Trenton and Asmara: The Red Sea Press, Inc.

Tomber, R. 2005. Aksumite and other imported ceramics from Kamrej. *Journal of Indian Ocean Archaeology* 2: 99-102.

Trimingham, Spencer. *Islam in Ethiopia.*

Tsehaye, Lalmba. 2008. Establishment and development of the national museum of Eritrea. In *Paleoanthropological and Archeo-Historical Research on Eritrea.* ed. Tekeste Melake. Asmara: National Museum of Eritrea.

Ullendorf, E. 1949. Note on the introduction of Christianity into Ethiopia. *Africa* 19.

– – – 1951. The Obelisk of Matara. *JRAS.*

Verma, Lal Bahadur. *Itihas Bodh.*

Wainwright, G. 1947. Early Foreign Trade in East Africa. *Man* 30.

– – – 1947. Early records of iron in Abyssinia. *Man* 30.

Walter, R. C., et al. 2000. Early human occupation of the Red Sea coast of Eritrea during the last interglacial. *Nature* 405: 65-69.

Wenig, S. 1997. German fieldwork in Eritrea. *Nyame Akuma* 48: 20-21.

– – – 2003. Enno Littmanns Deutsche Aksum-expedition 1906 und die German Archaeological Mission to Eritrea (G.A.M.E.) 90 Jahre spatter. *Nurnberger Blatter zur Archaologie* 18:79-98.

– – – 2006. Das Hochplateau von Qohaito: Impressionen. In *Kaiserlichem auftrag: Die deutsche Aksum-expedition 1906 unter Enno Liimann.* Forschungen zur Archaologie AuBereuropaischer Kulturen 3 (1): 353-362.

Woldemariam, Woldeab. 1987. *A Short History of Eritrea.* Oslo.

Woldemariam, Yebio. 1978. *Eritrea: Historical perspective.* New York.

Wolf, P. 1997. Preliminary report on the archaeological survey in Qohaito/ Eritrea. 1996. G.A.M.E. Manuscript.

Wolska-Conus, W. ed. 1968-73. *Cosmas indicopleustes. Topographie chretienne* (*Sources Chretienne 141, 159 and 197*). Paris: Editions du Cerf.

Zaborski, A. 1965. Notes on the medieval history of the Beja Tribes. *Foliaorientali* 7.

– – – 1967. Some remarks concerning Ezana's inscriptions and the Beja Tribes. *Folia Orientali* 9.

– – – 1970. Some Eritrean place names in Arabic medieval sources. *Folia orientali* 12.

– – – 1972. Beja and Tigre in the 9th and 10th c. period. *Rocznik orientalistyczny* 35 (1).

– – – 1984. Tigre and Bagulin in the 9th and 10th century period.

Zarins, Juris. 1988. Obsidian and the Red Sea trade: Prehistoric aspects. *Proceedings of ninth international congress of association of south Asian archaeologists in western Europe.* Venice.

Zemuy, Yonas. 2008. Eritrean rock art sites: A case study on rock art. . In *Paleoanthropological and Archeo-Historical Research on Eritrea.* ed. Tekeste Melake. Asmara: National Museum of Eritrea.

Index